Socialism
Re-examined

Books by Norman Thomas

A SOCIALIST'S FAITH

THE TEST OF FREEDOM

THE PREREQUISITES FOR PEACE

GREAT DISSENTERS

SOCIALISM RE-EXAMINED

NORMAN THOMAS

Socialism
Re-examined

NEW YORK

W·W·NORTON & COMPANY·INC·

Contents

	Preface	7
I	The World Socialism Faces	11
II	A Matter of Definition	25
III	Socialist Origins and Growth	32
IV	Socialism and Two World Wars	52
V	Communism	64
VI	Communism in the World	88
VII	Marxism's Inadequacies	101
VIII	Socialism in the U.S.A.	113
IX	Socialism in Mid-Century	131
X	Socialism Needs New Answers	150
XI	Socialism and Peace	161

5

XII   The Garrison State   183

XIII Socialism and the Emerging Nations   193

XIV   In Conclusion   208

      Appendix I
      (a) Aims and Tasks of Democratic
      Socialism   215
      ADOPTED AT THE FOUNDING CONGRESS OF THE
      SOCIALIST INTERNATIONAL AT FRANKFURT, GER-
      MANY, JULY, 1951

      (b) The World Today . . . The Socialist
      Perspective   224
      ADOPTED AT THE CONGRESS OF THE SOCIALIST IN-
      TERNATIONAL IN OSLO, 1962

      Appendix II
      Platform of Socialist Party, 1962   237

Preface

MY FIRST active work for the socialist cause began in 1917 when I campaigned for Morris Hillquit, the Socialist leader and mayoral candidate for New York City. I shall never forget the excitement and strain of my first outdoor campaign speech and of the mass meeting in the old Madison Square Garden, both without benefit of a then uninvented public address system. I little realized during those hectic days how much of my life was going to be devoted to socialism—its theory and its practice.

In the sixties, I thought it would be good for me, and, I hoped, for others, to examine, in some orderly fashion, the way in which the last forty tumultous years, as well as my own personal development, had affected my thinking about socialism. The result is this book. It has taken me longer to write than I had expected. Other activities had to come first, especially those connected with disarmament and peace. I have always thought that I was more effective as a speaker than as a writer, and so, when peace problems required my attention, writing gave way to speaking. Then, too, age has slowed my work.

7

It was inevitable that this book should have a personal quality. It was implicit in my apprehension of myself and of our times that it should raise more questions than it satisfactorily can answer. But I hope it proves that I am not adrift on an existentialist sea without chart or compass or desirable goal.

In expressing my views I have dealt rather summarily with ideas, issues and problems about which libraries have been and still are being written. What I have written is to be taken neither as socialist history nor as a dogmatic creed for socialism. Nor is it in any important respect a recantation of my earlier writings. It does not contradict, but brings up to date in observation and emphasis my book *A Socialist's Faith,* published in 1950.

I have inserted two appendices; one, giving the present official statement of the Socialist International and the other, the American Socialist Party's platform for 1962. The latter expands in detail certain of the proposals advanced in my book.

My manuscript went to the publisher at the end of February, 1963. Since then, there have been such important events as the publication of Pope John's encyclical, *Pacem in Terris,* his death, and the intensification of the ideological split and power conflict between the U.S.S.R. and China. Our government's policy in South Vietnam has become even harder to justify. The Negro protest has become a genuine mass revolution, so far still a comparatively nonviolent revolt, not against the American way of life, but for full incorporation in it. The stalemate on a treaty ending nuclear tests has been partially overcome by an agreement—still to be ratified by the Senate —ending tests in the atmosphere, upper space and the oceans. None of these events have changed my thinking on socialism for our times, but I rejoice that there has been a little progress since I completed the body of the book.

What does partially challenge my socialist thinking is Robert Theobald's argument in the *Nation*, May 11, 1963, that we have already come in America to a time when our capacity to produce with the aid of cybernetics makes it not only possible but necessary for the government to guarantee to us an income sufficient to enable each American to live with dignity. He makes a case not to be laughed off, but I think he underestimates the tremendous wrench in the popular ethic of work and responsibility which this would require. His theory is developed in terms of the advanced industrial nations and is scarcely applicable in the immense areas which are still under the economy of scarcity. Yet I think his thesis must receive sober consideration. This is not a revival of the untenable social credit plan.

Meanwhile my hope is that this book may point toward much further and faster progress in achieving human fraternity of action against war, poverty, aggression and hate.

Once more I acknowledge my indebtedness to my friend, associate, and secretary, Stephen Siteman, for his invaluable help. Books and articles by more writers than I can recall have helped to shape my opinions. Specific thanks are due to authors quoted and to the publishers who permitted me to quote them. They are identified in the text or by footnotes. And as always my thanks are due to my editors.

NORMAN THOMAS

Socialism
Re-examined

I.

The World
Socialism Faces

DEMOCRACY AND SOCIALISM, both, are ancient concepts. But as effective ideologies profoundly influencing human thought and practice, they are products of the Western world as it developed between the middle of the 18th century and the first world war. One can hardly reexamine either great ideology without first realizing that today's world is very different from the world of Adam Smith, Karl Marx, Edmund Burke or Thomas Jefferson.

In the first place, their world has both shrunk in size and expanded in complexity. We live, as we are now aware, on a minuscule planet in a small solar system in a universe wherein vast numbers of other planets may be homes of sentient beings, perhaps far more advanced than we. Ours is a world shrunk also by our achievements in communication and travel. Today one can fly from Washington to Delhi in far less time than one could travel from Washington to San Francisco in 1914.

Until 1914, this little earth was largely owned, or at

least controlled, by a handful of powerful nations or empires (all of them white except Japan). Now it is the home
of some 120 individually sovereign nation-states, all juridi-
cally equal, but with unequal distribution of area, population, wealth and military strength. Despite the frightful
cost in human life of two world wars, a population of
1,608,000,000 in 1900 had grown to a population of 2,971,-
800,000 (U.N. statistical office) by 1960. At the present
rate of increase, the population in the next century will
reach, according to Dr. Murray Luck, 9 billion. Allowing
that scientific methods, properly employed, will keep this
and an even larger population from starvation, our descendants will find themselves living in a dismally over-
crowded world where conflicting pressures of overpopulation will continually threaten peace and order. Nasser's
Egypt, for example, somehow must feed 500,000 additional mouths every year. The rate of increase will grow.
The great Aswan Dam project can do no more than miti-
gate the pressure. The India which Britain conquered was
on the average better fed than the free India over which
Nehru presides. Even its best economic planning cannot
greatly reduce a poverty and a level of unemployment for
which increasing overpopulation is largely responsible. Socialism's role remains to be discussed, but clearly no form
of socialism can be a substitute for birth control.

A second challenging problem is the disproportion between our material and spiritual development. Thanks to
our scientists, our control over natural forces and material
things has grown with breathtaking speed. But this growth
has been out of all proportion to the slower development
of that spirit of fraternity and those social institutions
which are essential if our newly won powers are to be used

to improve life rather than to facilitate death.

It was a hot war which enormously accelerated the development of atomic science for purposes of destruction. Today it is the Cold War which dominates the scientific field and dictates the nature and size of our expenditures of money and energy. There is a great and inspiring interest in exploring space, reaching the moon, and even at some distant time colonizing a remote planet. We want victory over space in peace but our budgets for its exploration are largely determined by a competition for military advantage in the anarchic rivalries of Great Powers. Modern medical knowledge has been a major cause of the population explosion. Thanks to today's sanitation and health measures, far fewer mothers lose their children to untimely death. But because we have failed to control births —a social failure—our medical triumphs contribute to disaster. We are able to build machines infinitely our superiors in the tasks for which they are made, but we tremble at the possible social consequences: "built-in" unemployment, and a leisure we do not know how to enjoy. We are trying to manage an economy of actual or potential surpluses with concepts developed under an economy of scarcity.

Eisenhower, Kennedy and Khrushchev have all declared nuclear war unthinkable. Yet so preempted are our energies by thinking about and preparing for just these wars that little time remains for solving the problems of the age of nuclear power and cybernetics. Americans and Russians have weapons enough to destroy life on this planet many times over, but we seek security—and in our America, employment—by restlessly piling up more. With our heads, if not with our hearts, we realize that, in the nuclear age,

the old and sometimes valid choice between war and freedom no longer holds. We must keep or win freedom in
peace—at least without nuclear war—for there will be no
freedom for the few and infinitely miserable survivors of
any atomic war. In short, we have made war between nuclear powers untenable at a time when, despite some small
progress in internationalism, the occasions for war have
been multiplied in the confused clash of ideologies, national ambitions and national economies.

A third important aspect of our changed world is the
rapid awakening of a large portion of mankind, most of
it belonging to races other than white, not only from political subservience to imperial powers, but from docile
acceptance of a poverty so complete as to make wholly
applicable Hobbes' old characterization of life as "poor,
nasty, brutish and short." The poverty against which European socialism revolted, offering a constructive remedy,
was never as great as that which still keeps two-thirds of
mankind on the narrow border line between chronic hunger and actual starvation. Anyone re-examining socialism
today is compelled to consider it as one answer to the
problem of lifting this curse from humanity, not only in
single nations but in the world.

National independence was a necessary first step in what
has been called "the revolution of rising expectations."
Political freedom from colonialism has been achieved
more easily and rapidly than anyone would have dreamed
in 1914.

The German colonial empire was smashed in World
War I. After Allied victory in World War II the British
Labor Party, to the everlasting credit of its socialism, be-
gan the peaceful and friendly dissolution of the Empire.

The United States had set a good example by fulfilling its promise of independence to the Philippines. The process has gone on. The dominant white European nations had neither the desire nor the capacity to maintain the old imperialisms which, by and large, no longer afforded them great economic returns. Rather the contrary was the case. Russia alone has expanded her empire since World War II, but under the pretext of communism's concern for freeing her satellites from capitalist bondage.

It is already clear that national freedom in most of the new nations—and in some of the old—does not mean individual freedom as Western democrats have understood it. The people themselves are concerned for more bread and a little cake rather than for the right "to know, to utter and argue freely, according to conscience," for what we Americans call civil liberties. The desire for this freedom has come late in the history of mankind. Conformity to the group interests and mores has been a necessary requirement for holding the favor of tribal gods or for national survival and economic progress. Nkrumah of Ghana, for example, has felt it necessary not only to create for himself the image of a glorified tribal chief but to deal sternly with potential rivals and critics. The rights he demanded from the British he does not extend to his countrymen. Unity, he insists, is necessary to build his nation, and unity requires a high degree of submission to him, his ideas and his program. In Cuba, Castro's affection for freedom is shown by his acceptance of the communist travesty on it.

What Robert Heilbroner calls *The Great Ascent* will require more and better economic aid to emerging nations from their more affluent neighbors. But that is only part

of the story. The ascent cannot be made by imitating
America's history of economic growth. It will not be a
matter of a few years. It will probably require authoritarian government dedicated to some type of socialist or
collective economy. What will, what should be the Western democratic, especially democratic socialist, attitude
toward an ascent which, as Mr. Heilbroner believes, will
be harsh, often violent, and oppressive? No democratic
socialist can escape this problem. Neither socialism nor
democracy can be triumphant if practiced by a few nations only.

In this challenging world the principal religion is the
religion of nationalism. It is a religion which shows itself
at its worst when its god, the nation-state, tries to extend
its rule over other peoples. As a religion this cult of the
sovereign nation-state is amoral. Most rulers would have
to echo what the Italian Liberal statesman, Cavour, wrote
toward the end of his life to a friend: "We should have
been great rascals if we had done for ourselves what we
have done for Italy." It is the sovereign nation-state (as I
have told many audiences) which in our day tells us: "I
am the Lord, thy God. Thou shalt have no other gods
before me. Thou shalt not take my name in vain, for thy
rulers will not hold him guiltless that taketh my name in
vain. Thou shalt not kill—retail. Thou shalt not refuse to
kill wholesale at my demand. Thou shalt not bear false
witness against thy neighbor—unless for my power and
glory."

This religion lives by its fears and hates as well as by
its loves. Human beings and their loyalties have developed
in groups. Their *we* demands a *they*. The group to which
we men give chief loyalty, that is, for which we have been

willing to kill or die, has slowly grown from clan to nation.

To reject the religion of nationalism is not to reject the right sort of patriotism. He is peculiarly insensitive who does not feel a love of his country—a love which can be beautiful and rewarding. This love has inspired literature and the arts, to our enrichment. To ask us to scrap our national loyalties for one world-state is to ask what is presently impossible.

If such a switch were possible, it would be at the price of wholesome variety and probably—at least at first—of individual freedom. But it is a bad way of cherishing one's own nation to set its supposed interests above the moral law.

What is wrong is that our 120 sovereign nation-states live in an anarchic world, without recognized law; that they assert themselves most zealously in terms of military power; that they easily sanctify any violence or deceit which may advance that power. Socialism has provided no automatic answer to the religion of absolute nationalism. It usually coexists with it. And so, increasingly, in its own way, does communism.

The revealed religions—Judaism, Islam, Hinduism, and Christianity, in its Protestant and Catholic forms—have long since made their peace on various terms with the states wherein they are strong.* Once our worst wars were religious, fought over the "road to heaven" and the claims of rival churches to power on earth. That era has mostly ended, partly because the religion of nationalism has taken first place, partly because religious tolerance

---

* Max Weber and R. H. Tawney have shown the relation of the churches to prevailing economies, the Catholic especially to the feudal and the Protestant to the capitalist.

and concern for human well-being have increased. Yet in our time there are tragic exceptions to this generalization.

The establishment of Israel, that little nation which is in many ways so admirable, cannot be explained without reference to the Jewish religion, no matter how many Zionists may be atheists or agnostics. Alas, the establishment of this refuge for Jews from gentile hostility meant the dispossession of hundreds of thousands of Arabs from Palestine. Thus, Islam, in the Middle East, now plays a more intolerant role than before: while in support of Arab states, she has been unable, as yet, to unite them in much more than hate of Israel.

Even worse proof of the continuing strength of religion as a divisive force among men has been furnished in India, the India of that great apostle of nonviolence, Mohandas Gandhi. One cannot explain solely in terms of conflicting religious practices and doctrines the horrible violence of both Moslem and Hindu—and the mass migrations on both sides—at the time of the partition of the Indian subcontinent into India and Pakistan. But neither can one explain it without understanding how mighty among the populace were the religious differences which Jinnah and others manipulated in the service of their religion of nationalism. Jinnah himself was a very free-thinking Moslem, but he stood out as defender of the Moslem faith.

In the West, since the Nazi horror, there has been a diminution of anti-Semitism, and certainly less justification for it by Christian churches. The relations of Catholics and Protestants, especially under the late Pope John XXIII, have greatly improved.

Karl Marx, and indeed all his contemporary socialists,

would have been surprised had they been able to foresee
the improved stands for social justice taken by Roman
Catholics and leading Protestant churches of today. Although these churches must, in general, still be ranked
among the conservative antisocialist forces, they are no
longer everywhere to be counted as major defenders of
the status quo. Except for its routine criticism of "socialism," and its opposition to birth control, Pope John's
encyclical, *Mater et Magistra*, compares favorably with
most democratic socialist platforms, and the platforms or
declarations of certain Catholic political parties in some
countries would astonish the clerical parties of the mid-
nineteenth century. In the vital issue of school integration
in the U.S.A. the episcopal power has in many areas put
parochial schools in the vanguard of those accepting the
Supreme Court's decisions. (The Catholic insistence that
children of Catholics attend parochial schools is in itself,
however, an undesirable form of segregation.)

In the major Protestant churches the social gospel may
not furnish the rallying cry to a concerned minority to
the degree that it did during the "good years" before
World War I, but at least on paper the official declarations
of the governing bodies of the churches show far wider
acceptance of it. They also show somewhat more concern
for peace. After the Armistice in 1918 one of the leading
officials of a church peace movement rejected my plea for
Molokan religious conscientious objectors, who were man-
acled in a standing position eight hours a day in solitary
cells in Ft. Leavenworth, on the theory that they were
barely better than traitors. I finally got help outside the
churches (mostly from the N.Y. *World*). That sort of
thing could hardly happen today.

This description of the world in which socialism must be assayed has already contained reference to the Cold War with its arm race. The fact of the Cold War underlies and colors all our thinking. It is, as I have suggested, partly the result of a clash of national interests much as were the wars of old. But it is also in men's minds a clash of ideologies, communism vs. democracy, which somewhat resembles older wars of religion. Democratic socialism, as we shall see, has been caught between its devotion to democracy and its general historic sympathy with the social and economic order which communism seeks, but defiles, by its totalitarian tactics. Here it is necessary to point, somewhat sadly, to the weakness of the democratic faith in the minds of many of its advocates. There is a widespread and lamentable tendency to make the noble word, "free," simply a synonym for noncommunist—thus Spain, Portugal, and Saudi Arabia are "free" nations. The loudest critics of communism in the imperfectly democratic countries of the West are rarely conspicuous as defenders of civil rights regardless of color and of civil liberties here in America. Better men than they are often inclined to agree with Winston Churchill's observation that democracy is a poor form of government but that everything else is worse—scarcely a fighting declaration of faith.

Which leads to the judgment that our present age is sick with frustration. At our high point of triumph over our physical environment we tend to be cynical or to despair about ourselves—or at any rate about our neighbors. At this point popular Freudianism is of no help. The question is, are we human beings capable of the rationality and effective fraternity upon which a good life, perhaps even our escape from the collective suicide of nuclear war, depends?

This pessimism about ourselves, this acceptance of irrationality, this wallowing in our low spiritual estate, finds expression in our culture—our music, our art and our literature.

In the magazine, *Horizon,* July, 1962, Alfred Kazin told his interviewers: "There is a pervasive uncertainty that finds a home in the university and in safe specialties." This is hardly a basis for socialist progress. Still less help is to be found in the men—so numerous in many of our novels and in life—who defend themselves "in the frivolous fashion of our society by pretending that there is nothing to believe in." (Again the quotation is from Kazin.)

In the same issue of *Horizon* Frank Gettern wonders about the significance of the fact that "a note common to all our official art is violent disorder, whether it is that of spilled paint or that of junked automobiles." So he describes many of the pictures hanging not only on the walls of museums but in the executive offices of great corporations.

I know modern novels mostly through their reviews, but if I thought that they portrayed the true state of mankind, I should doubt our capability of achieving a social order worth saving. Too many think we are all, at best, passengers on Katherine Anne Porter's *Ship of Fools.* It is a sick humanity which revels in sexuality, on the screen, and in the books of Henry Miller, William Burroughs and others of that ilk. Juvenile delinquency, which concerns us so much is, in part, the consequence of our slums, but it abounds also where there is no such easy economic explanation. I think that the current mixture of apathy, amorality and lack of purpose can be very largely explained by the conflict of fear and hate inflicted on us by the Cold War.

This pessimism about us moderns is partly the reason Senator Barry Goldwater, *et al.*, if rather absurdly, find an American utopia in the past—let us say in the time of William McKinley. A popular historian, Walter Lord, writing about the early years of this century, has called them the Good Years. And so they were in my recollection. But not because social conditions in America were better than they are today. Those were years of child labor and of unorganized workers, grossly exploited and working long hours for very low wages. There was only the beginning of a conscience about the second-class citizenship—or worse—of the Negro. But they were good years because it was possible to believe in relatively simple cures for particular problems. We were full of hope. Socialist enthusiasts for Gene Debs expected to live to march in triumph at his inauguration. Liberal or progressive reformers were confident of early victory. We were believers in Progress with a capital "P." Our confident hopes were shattered in the wholly unexpected war into which the United States was drawn. The hysterical illusion that it would make the world safe for democracy was soon shattered.

Indeed we have been inclined to go too far in our disillusionment. We expected too much too easily and in our disappointment we fell back on apathy, an amoral scramble for money and status, a rather cheap cynicism, or a worship of strength as strength, no matter how employed. We invited the coming of the theater of the absurd.

The case is not hopeless. Leave out war, and the po-

litical-economic progress of mankind in my lifetime has
been great. Because we must believe that human failings
are as much a cause as a result of an unjust social order,
we are not doomed to despair.

We have a significant beginning of a sound internationalism in the U.N., some inadequacies of its charter
notwithstanding. The Marshall Plan—and now the Peace
Corps—have had no precedent in the history of nations
and their mutual relations. Here at home, disgraced as we
are by racism in Mississippi and in many other places
besides, we can believe that at last we are shaking off the
terrible legacy of a more terrible chattel slavery and putting into effect the egalitarian principle we have professed.
Organized labor has disappointed many starry-eyed expectations. It has not proved that the workers, given well
established rights, would almost automatically renounce
"bourgeois" prejudices and "bourgeois" corruptions. Unions have not accomplished what socialists had hoped.
But no one, remembering the "good old days" of long
hours, unsafe working conditions, low wages, strikes of
desperation, can help but say, thank God for the unions.

Civil liberties are always threatened; they certainly
are threatened now, as is our whole democracy, by our
descent toward a garrison state under pressure from what
Eisenhower called the military-industrial complex. Yet,
by and large, civil liberties and civil rights have gained,
not lost, since World War I. Even a garrison state today
must be something of a welfare state.* Our mismanage-

* The current distinction between civil rights, that is, against racial
and other discriminations between citizens, and civil liberties, against
denials of abridgement of freedom of religion, speech, the press, assembly
and association, seems to me unfortunate, even though I use it here in
describing the present situation.

ment of an interdependent world has been abundantly proved, but we are learning, if slowly, to manage it far better. At least Hitler and Stalin are gone.

The worst of us is copy for journalists and novelists. The best of us makes dull reading: it has the distinction of being taken for granted. We could not have gotten where we are had it not been for the existence and persistence, yes, even the growth, of an essential goodness and a capacity for fraternal cooperation on which our future depends. Men do not work exclusively for power and profit.

Certainly there is no guarantee that we men can solve the problems we ourselves have made. War in a nuclear age is still more likely than peace. But there are in men qualities that make possible a better future. Can socialism draw out these qualities and give them expression before it is too late?

II.

A Matter of Definition

ALL GREAT concepts, democracy, Christianity, socialism, are less than self-defining. Their various supporters
explain them quite differently. So do their critics. Socialism suffers especially from this lack of definitiveness, and
from the emotions which attend its various interpretations. To communists, socialism is something already
achieved in the Soviet Union as a major step toward the
near-perfect communist society. To democratic socialists,
socialism is the strongest and most consistent alternative
to communist totalitarian repression. In the United States
socialism is generally a bad word, while capitalism—
nowadays, usually called, or miscalled, "free enterprise"
—is a good one. In most of the rest of the world socialism
tends to be the good word and capitalism the bad one.

This variety of definitions was amusingly demonstrated
on a radio panel discussion a few years ago in which I
took part. Miss Vivian Kellems, a "free enterprise" cru-
sader, told us that socialism began in the United States

when William Howard Taft proclaimed the adoption of
the income tax amendment to the Constitution. Another
member of the panel was disposed to challenge my right
to call myself a socialist, although I had been the nominee
of the Socialist Party six times for the presidency. I wasn't
Marxist enough.

An outstanding sociologist, Daniel Bell, entitled a valuable collection of essays, *The End of Ideology,* and in
a sense his title describes the intellectual development, or
lack of it, in American social and political theory after
World War II. During Khrushchev's first visit to the
United States, he carried on a running argument with
various businessmen or their spokesmen, both sides speaking in terms largely unrelated to the realities of the systems they were championing. It would be interesting to
hear the comments of Adam Smith and Karl Marx, raised
from the dead, on the present systems which honor them.
A very competent economist of my acquaintance says that
the only practitioners of genuine laissez faire "free enterprise" in the United States are boys playing marbles for
keeps: they have no tariffs, parity payments, government
subsidies, guaranteed collective bargaining—only their
marbles.

For myself, I shall consider socialism rather inclusively,
describing it in its various aspects rather than precisely
defining it. I shall have to take into account the communist
theory of it as a state on the way to the social bliss of
communism, but I shall be more concerned with democratic socialism as it is understood and, when feasible,
practiced by the parties associated in the Socialist International.

This socialism has become, in practice, a pragmatic

affair, but it commonly emphasizes, especially since World War II, its ethical aspect. "The starting point of all socialist thought," the British Socialist Union declared, "has been the condemnation of capitalist exploitation." It goes on to say that "the essence of socialism is the perpetual struggle to realize its ideals" which ideals involve the human spirit. Therefore their fulfillment is a matter involving not only changes in the social structure but in human attitudes as well. "There is no accepted institutional blueprint called socialism."

Writing in "Images of Socialism" in the American journal, *Dissent,* Lewis Coser and Irving Howe begin by quoting Tolstoy's remarkable statement, "God is the name of my desire." They go on to say: "Without sanctioning the facile identification that is frequently made between religion and socialist politics, we should like to twist Tolstoy's remark to our own ends: 'Socialism is the name of our desire.' " They then discuss the possibility of specifying what the socialist desire means or should mean.

Socialists often define that desire in terms of the great generalities: freedom, equality, fellowship. But thus to describe it is to lose distinctive meaning for socialism in a sea of noble generalities not exclusively socialist property. In his important book, *The Economics of Socialism Reconsidered,* Henry Smith, vice principal of Ruskin College, Oxford, makes a good case against so indefinitely defining or describing socialism. He reminds us that capitalist exploitation isn't self-defining. It can only be given meaning in economic terms. " 'Freedom' as a word has no meaning except in so far as it is tied down to 'freedom *from* this' or 'freedom *to* that.' Freedom from exploitation negates 'freedom to exploit'; the discussion immediately moves back into economic grounds." Therefore, Mr. Smith concludes: "Socialism can be most usefully defined as the demand for minimization of conflict arising out of economic relationships."

It is a definition which I very much like, but one must understand what the author means by economic. He quotes approvingly Wicksteed in *The Common Sense of Political Economy:*

"A vast range, therefore, of our relations with others enters into a system of mutual adjustment by which we further each other's purposes simply as an indirect way of furthering our own. All such relations may be fitly called 'economic.' . . . I define my relations with any other man as 'economic' when I enter into it for this purpose of transmuting, either at one or at two or at more removes, what I have and can into what I want and would . . . If you and I are conducting a transaction which on my side is purely economic, I am furthering your purposes, partly or wholly perhaps for my own sake, perhaps entirely for the sake of others, but certainly not for your sake. What makes it an economic transaction is that I am not considering you except as a link in the chain, or considering your desires except as the means by which I may gratify those of someone else—not necessarily myself. The economic relation does not exclude from my mind everyone but me, it potentially includes everyone but you. You it does indeed exclude, and therefore it emphasizes, though it does not narrow or tighten, the limitation of the altruism of the man who enters into it; for it calls our attention to the fact that, however wide his sympathies may be, they do not urge him to any particular effort or sacrifice for the sake of the person with whom he is dealing at the moment. An economic relation may be entered upon equally well from egoistic or altruistic motives; but as long as it remains purely economic, it must remind us that no man's altruism is undiscriminating to the extent of lavishing itself upon all persons or all purposes at all times."

It is possible, of course, to accept this definition without becoming a narrow economic determinist. Mr. Smith, in developing his definition of socialism in economic terms, has much to say about the political applications of his definition. He nowhere equates it with the narrow, school-dictionary definition of socialism as a doctrine of public ownership of all, or of the principal, means of production and distribution—an incorrect oversimplification which much socialist propaganda has seemed to invite. But he does insist that advocacy of some form or forms of social ownership has been the most characteristic feature of socialism.

Nevertheless, while I shall keep this economic definition of socialism in mind, I do not expect to use it often in popular speaking or writing. Not without considerable expansion and explanation. It does not, to the average man, suggest the depth of socialist concern for a philosophy of history—Marx worked out his before he developed his economics—or its involvement in the politics of nationalism and internationalism. Still less does it suggest the driving power of the ethical demand for justice and fellowship which has constrained men to consider ways to minimize conflict and end human exploitation. Mr. Smith himself lessens the value of his definition by saying:

"The watershed of ideas between the communist and non-communist world is the conviction of the former that the capitalist form of economic life is a phase in the development of human society which must inevitably be ephemeral, either collapsing into chaos or suffering a revolutionary transmi-

gration into socialism. If this be true, then all disregard of
human rights, all sacrifice of the present generation for
future ones, all distortion of lesser truth, can be justified, because what is at stake is the maintenance and development
of the whole fabric of civilization. If this be sincerely believed to be true (and all history shows the tragic power of
human conviction) then the difference between the two
armed camps in the shadow of which our generation lives is
not a difference of moral values nor of intellectual integrity,
but a difference in the premise from which evaluation and
logic commence."

There is no tenable theory of morals or logic which can
hold that "all disregard of human rights, all sacrifice of
the present generation, all distortion of lesser truth, can
be justified" by the dogmatic conviction, however sincere,
that such action is necessary to maintain and develop the
fabric of civilization. What kind of civilization can triumph by these means? Mr. Smith does not accept this
Bolshevik premise but his economic definition of socialism ought not to make room for its acceptance in any
popular theory of morals or politics. Therefore, I repeat
that, important and helpful as Mr. Smith's definition is,
our re-examination of socialism cannot be so much in
terms of its conformity to his definition as of socialists'
own claims, their sometimes conflicting dogmas or interpretations of them, and their own record of performance,
in our violent and confused world. An old dispute among
socialists, shall our approach be scientific or ethical?,
should be—indeed has been—dropped by most democratic socialists. It must be both.

With this understanding, I should not too much quarrel
with the Merriam-Webster dictionary definition of

socialism: "A political and economic theory of social organization the essential feature of which is governmental control of economic activities to the end that competition shall give way to cooperation, and that the opportunities of life and the rewards of labor shall be equitably apportioned." But it is a definition needing descriptive application in the light of socialism's history and present status.

III.

Socialist Origins
and Growth

THE ROOTS of socialism are planted deep in the evolution of human society. Many of them, despite Marx, are religious and ethical. But then, religion and ethics themselves have been greatly affected by the way men have made their living, each in his own society. Max Beer, in his fascinating *General History of Socialism and Social Struggles*, argues, for example, that the biblical conflict between Jehovah and his prophets and Baal was a conflict between a god of the desert and the gods of the Canaanites in the more fertile areas. This is, I think, true, but it is not the whole explanation of Amos' lofty, ethical monotheism. What is certain is that Jewish and Christian socialisms can find plenty of effective texts in their scriptures. "Where your treasure is there will your heart be also" was not said by a socialist economic determinist.

It is well known that the early Christians had all things in common. The history of Christianity is studded with recurring efforts of Christians to challenge exploitation by

32

church and state and to form their own more or less com-
munistic communities.

But one does not have to believe in the infallibility of
Karl Marx to agree with him that socialism as a successful
system of production for the benefit of the human family,
rather than for the profit of a relatively few, required the
productive capacity, and the discipline of workers, which
came with the industrial revolution—let us say, with
James Watt's patent of the steam engine in 1775.

G. D. H. Cole begins his authoritative *History of
Socialist Thought* with the French Revolution. Not because the French Revolution itself was socialist. Rather
it marked the rise to power of the middle class, and, with
it, a troubled victory of democracy. There was, however,
a socialist episode during the French Revolution: Gracchus Babeuf led the Conspiracy of Equals in the first
attempt to make socialism a practical policy for the state.
Babeuf's conspiracy was rapidly repressed. But Mr. Cole
chooses to begin with the Revolution less because of
Babeuf than because, as he writes, "What the French
Revolution did was, not to bring Socialism into force as
a living and continuous social movement, but rather by
developing for the first time into a political struggle the
antagonism between the rich and poor and substituting
this antagonism for the earlier antagonisms between the
privileged and unprivileged classes, to set the stage for
the long-drawn-out social struggles of nineteenth century
Europe, out of which the modern Socialist movement
arose." In America, on the eve of the French Revolution,
James Madison, one of our founding fathers, wrote (in
the *Federalist*), "Those who hold and those who are
without property have ever formed distinct interests in

society." Not quite the doctrine of class struggle, but on
the way.

The socialist movement would have exhausted itself
in violent protest had workers in the Western world not
been persuaded that science and technology—and full
value for their toil—would allow them to share abundance.
Moreover, during and after the French Revolution, they,
with uneven progression, acquired the use of democracy's
political tools from a reluctant middle class which was
constrained by the logic of its own claims against feudalism and the crown, and by pressure from the workers, to
share civil liberties and representative institutions. This
was of great importance in the development of democratic socialism.

The process by which capitalism made industrial workers out of craftsmen and peasants was grim. Hours were
long, and wages were so low that children were forced
to go to the factories instead of to schools. A great many
workers lost the satisfaction of making any sort of whole
object of beauty or use; factory hands and their families
were crowded into ugly slums in smoke-drenched air.
Their new lot set them in far sharper opposition to the
entrepreneurs or to the owner of the tools than under
the older guild system. Yet, there was a feeling of progress
in the air; the workers were, or could be, convinced that
they and their children were not forever bound to a hopeless wage slavery under a brutal capitalist system.

The leaders in the development of socialism were almost
all rebels from the upper and intellectual classes. (Why,
is a problem that much interests the psychological school
of interpretation.) The Rochdale tailors and workers—
organized as consumers who started a great consumers'

cooperative—stood out because they functioned without a Fourier, a Marx, a Lassalle, a Bakunin. Labor unions, necessarily concerned first with immediate problems, arose from the ranks of the workers. But they also owed much to middle-class intellectuals and dissenters. They were products of the industrial revolution more than of any theory, but on the European continent they were generally avowedly socialist.

The list of 19th century apostles of revolution and formulators of socialist theory—or theories, for they were often in conflict—is long, but Marx towers above them in his intellectual achievement and persistent influence. Marx did not invent socialism. Nor is Marxism synonymous with socialism. There were socialists long before Marx, and many socialists who were active during and after his lifetime were not Marxists. Professed Marxists often differed sharply in their interpretations of his writings. There would have been, I think, a strong socialist movement of some sort without Marx, but unquestionably he, aided by his friend, financial supporter and collaborator, Friedrich Engels, stood out above all others as the philosopher and apostle of socialism.

Marx was a man of unusual learning, a philosopher— originally a Hegelian, he "stood Hegelianism on its head" —a scientific analyst of history, a sociologist, an economist. To socialism, he gave intellectual self-confidence and a sense of destiny. According to Marx, history ordained that working men, having won the class struggle, would establish an economy based on social ownership and production so abundant that ultimately wealth would be distributed on the principle, "from every man according to his ability; to every man according to his need." I shall try briefly to state the essence of Marxism, returning later to discuss its adequacy to our times.

Central to Marx's theory was his doctrine of the class struggle. It was intertwined with his philosophy of the materialist conception of history and with his economic Theory of Value and Surplus Value. The political theory of the dictatorship of the proletariat—the essential form of government during the transition from the state, organ of capitalism, to the stateless society of communism— acquired immense importance as it was developed by Lenin and Stalin, but was not elaborated or much discussed by Marx. In the acrimonious debates among socialists which accompanied the rise of Bolshevism to power, such loyal Marxists as Kautsky, Lenin, and Rosa Luxemburg could give it very different meanings.

The most widely read and discussed brief formulation of the class-struggle doctrine is to be found in Marx's *Communist Manifesto* of 1848. It reads:

"The history of all hitherto existing society is the history of class struggles.

"Freeman and slave, patrician and plebeian, lord and serf, guild-master and journeyman, in a word; oppressor and oppressed, stood in constant opposition to one another, carried on uninterrupted now hidden, now open fight, fight that each time ended, either in a revolutionary reconstitution of society at large, or in the common ruin of the contending classes.

"In the earlier epochs of history, we find almost everywhere a complicated arrangement of society into various orders, a manifold gradation of social rank. In ancient Rome, we have patricians, knights, plebeians, slaves; in the Middle Ages, feudal lords, vassals, guild-masters, journeymen, apprentices, serfs; in almost all these classes, again, subordinate gradations . . .

"Our epoch, the epoch of the bourgeoisie, possesses, however, this distinctive feature; it has simplified the class antagonisms. Society as a whole is more and more splitting up into two great hostile camps, into two great classes directly facing each other: Bourgeoisie and Proletariat."

Marx believed that the victory of the proletariat was ordained by history, but yet he insisted that victory could be won only after a struggle. Mankind must pass through a bitter period of increasing misery during which large numbers of the middle class would be forced into the ranks of the working class—the masses of factory workers. Marx held that, along with inevitable capitalist consolidation, there "grows the mass of misery, oppression, slavery, degradation, exploitation. But with this grows too the revolt of the working class, a class always increasing in numbers, and disciplined, united, organized by the very mechanics of the process of capitalist production itself."

Along with this theory and his theory of value and surplus value, Marx stated a Theory of Recurring Crises of unemployment and suffering. Such crises, he held, are inherent in the capitalist system. They are due not to overproduction but to underconsumption. These crises ultimately will paralyze the system which, as socialists (before Keynes had developed his ideas) liked to say, would "suffocate in its own fat." To thousands of workers this theory seemed to be borne out by the Great Depression of the nineteen thirties.

Though Marx made the Materialist Conception of History the warp of all his thinking, he never systematically expounded its meaning. In its simplest form, it is the doctrine which holds economic forces predominant in the direction of social affairs, not as G. D. H. Cole, writing on

Marx in the *Encyclopaedia Britannica*, correctly explains, the doctrine that individual men act only from material motives.

"In essence,"

Cole writes,

"Marx contended that there exist, in any society, certain material 'forces of production' and a certain knowledge of their use in man's service. These form the 'conditions of production,' and for their employment there is required an arrangement of the powers of society, implying a certain relationship among the members, and the establishment and maintenance of appropriate social institutions. If, for example, at a particular state of development the 'forces of production' are to be fully exploited, certain forms of private property must be recognized and secured, and certain members of society endowed with authority both over the material means of production and over the other members, who must accept the subordinate role assigned to them by the dictates of economic circumstance. This recognition and this authority imply and require a power able to enforce them; and this power is found in the State, which takes its special form from the character of the economic institutions it exists to uphold. Political and social institutions are thus dependent upon, and derive their special forms from, the underlying economic circumstances of the society in which they exist. Political power is a derivative power, depending for its validity and survival on its correspondence with the needs forced on men by the conditions of production.

"These underlying conditions are, however, flexible because of changes both in the forces of production at men's command in the knowledge of their use. It follows that the superstructure—the arrangement of social classes and the political institutions by which the existing order is maintained—must also change as the conditions of production are

modified. But institutions, once established, are highly re-
sistant to modification. The class-structure of society and its
political and social institutions therefore tend to lag behind
the movement of economic change, until the accumulated
disharmony forces drastic readjustment by the method of
revolution. Then the entire superstructure is brought crash-
ing down, and a new arrangement of classes and a new set
of institutions in harmony with the new economic order
arise."

It is, of course, the working class which will be the
instrument for bringing to an end a capitalist system
which no longer corresponds to the conditions of production. Hence the vital importance of the class struggle.

It remains to summarize briefly the doctrine of Value
and Surplus Value. It is the main theme of Volume I of
Das Kapital and recurs in somewhat different shape in
Volume III, published from Marx's notes after his death.
Socialist economists still argue whether the latter treatment is a development or a modification of the former.
Socialist writers, before Marx, basing their arguments on
Ricardo's doctrine that the value of commodities depends
upon the amount of labor involved in their production,
had held that workers were entitled to the whole produce
of labor, and that rent, profit and interest which went to
capitalists were simply extorted by the capitalists' power
in the community. Again to quote Cole:

"Marx refines upon this view, and seeks to show that the
extortion is made possible because, whereas all commodities
sell at their value (apart from temporary market deviations)
there is one peculiarity about the worker's only commodity,
his labor-power, that marks it off from all others. For this
commodity alone has the power, in producing other commodities, to produce a value greater than it possesses itself.

The value of the commodity, labor-power, is determined, like that of all other commodities, by the quantity of labor required for its production, or in other words, by the amount of labor required to enable the laborer to subsist and re-produce his kind. But the laborer produces by a day's work more than enough for his subsistence and the subsistence of his family. The capitalist, after paying him a subsistence wage, is able to keep for himself the rest of the laborer's product. This residue, the fund from which rent, interest and profits are drawn, Marx calls 'surplus value.' Suppose, he says, the laborer works 12 hours a day, and only 6 hours are needed for his subsistence. The capitalist can then filch in the form of surplus value the product of 6 hours' labor. The rate of surplus value is 100 per cent of the laborer's wage, and 50 per cent of the total product."

There are complexities in this theory. It does not mean that each worker can or should receive the full value of his own product. The economic system is a whole. It is the working *class* which is exploited. Moreover, Marx recognized a difference between socially useful and so-cially useless work and of course he knew that the workers needs tools for production. In *Das Kapital* he introduces his concept of variable and constant capital. The former is spent on labor; the latter is spent on machinery, etc.— hardly "constant" in the usual sense of the word, es-pecially in an age of automation. Moreover he maintains that not all commodities sell at their value. They sell at prices from which capitalist owners can get profit and the relation of profit to surplus value is complex.

One can learn how a modern socialist economist looks at Marx's theory from Henry Smith's *The Economics of Social-ism Reconsidered*. For myself I have never quite understood the place it held in socialist discussions in the 19th century except that it was a very learned way to tell the workers that they were robbed and therefore could claim the right to expropriate the expropriators. That is an important exception. Sidney Hook has suggested that Marx's theory was the way things looked to the workers in the middle of the last century. I doubt, perhaps unfairly, that many rank and file socialists, after painfully wading through *Das Kapital*, got from Marx's learned presentation very much more than a sense of justification to end capitalist exploitation. Both his historical and economic theories led Marx to believe that more and more of the middle class would be forced into the proletariat. Capitalism would increase the total of human misery. This has been called the theory of immiseration.

Marx's was a greatness of the mind, not of the personality. In his earlier years he was concerned by the alienation of the individual in society. He made men face the consequences to the individual of a capitalist economy whose work, he thought, was nearly done. He was a dedicated man, but he was not a great lover of his kind; that is, of human beings as human beings. He set a bad example to his followers in his controversial tactics, for instance, against Bakunin. One of his biographers, Otto Rühle, writes, "In that world of concrete reality, Marx failed no less utterly than he triumphed in the realm of abstract intelligence. His failure was as pitiful in the one as his success was magnificent in the other. Essentially, however, there is no opposition to these two phenomena."

Mr. Rühle goes so far as to suggest to the reader that the methods used by Marx in developing his theories constituted compensation for an inferiority complex, and that without it and the faults which flowed from it, we

might never have had socialism! I am not denying some
merit to this psychological theory of compensation when
I say that Marx's gifts to socialism would have been even
greater had he himself been a better exemplar of the type
of man socialism might produce. Anyway, socialism was
not born of one man's inferiority complex, nor of that
passion for power which, as Max Nomad has shown,
possessed most of the great radical heretics.

Marx could not possibly have done what he did without the constant and patient financial support and intellectual collaboration of his friend, Friedrich Engels.

Marx is so connected with socialism that many non-
socialists believe that international socialism derived directly and incontrovertibly from his famous *Communist
Manifesto*. That is not the case. Marx did his great work
while living in England, but it has been said that the
socialism of the British Labor Party (which came late to
open avowal of socialism) owed more to Methodism than
to Marx. It also owed much to Fabian gradualist socialism
preached by a society to which such notables as George
Bernard Shaw and the Webbs belonged. The British
Independent Labor Party pioneered in Labor's espousal
of socialism. It was radical but less purely Marxist than
many contemporary parties. Keir Hardy was its notable
leader. The present Labor Party grew out of labor unions.
It was immensely stimulated early in this century, by
legislation and court decisions harmful to union interests.

Marxism had its troubles on the European Continent,
where socialism was long less avowedly Marxist than it
had become just before the first world war. The movement
was complex and various. Socialists were divided by
controversy—some personal, some ideologic. Several

basic philosophies coexisted within the movement, neither easily woven together, nor yet easily eliminated.

At the end of his monumental history, G. D. H. Cole, in a chapter entitled "Looking Backwards and Forewards," finds four distinct lines of thought, running like strands through the evolution of socialism, from its beginnings at the end of the 19th century to the outbreak of World War II.

The first strand he finds in Gracchus Babeuf and his Conspiracy of the Equals of 1796, first of a series of insurrectionary risings by a devoted revolutionary elite, the Socialist Conspirators, directed to greater equality. Here, too, Cole includes the two French socialists, Blanqui and Barbes, the Paris Commune of 1870, and "in certain aspects" the leaders of the Bolshevik Revolution of 1917. In most socialist discussion this socialism is called Blanquist, after the French revolutionist of the 1848 period.

The second strand arose with the early community-projectors—with the British, Robert Owen, and the French, Charles Fourier. With different appeals both urged the formation of small communities, "withdrawn from the competition around them to pursue the good life in little, for the most part self-sufficient groups of producer-consumers, cooperating instead of contending for the means of living and animated by social philosophies of mutual good will." Marx called them utopian. The idea of socialist communities was almost played out by the beginning of the 20th century—except in Israeli kibbutzim. But among many socialists the decentralizing influence, the fear of big central government, persisted.

Third was Henri Saint-Simon, "a planner with a considered doctrine of historical development." Saint-Simon

hoped that the various classes would collaborate to end
war and exploitation, and would plan to increase social
wealth by leaps and bounds. The planning would be
authoritarian; inheritance would be abolished. Though
Saint-Simon's school disappeared, its influence has persisted: Cole traces back to Saint-Simon that strand of
thinking "which ranges Socialism with the advocates of
planned economy, and also the tendency which ranges it
on the side of technological development and large scale
industrialism as the necessary foundations of a Socialist
order."

The fourth major strand in socialism's turbulent history
came from the works of Louis Blanc in France and of
Ferdinand Lassalle in Germany. (At the time of his death,
the latter was, in Germany, one of Marx's rivals for the
role of Master-teacher.) Blanc, in the eighteen-forties
advocated "self-governing national workshops, to be established and financed by a reformed democratic state,
but left free to manage their own affairs subject only to
a general coordinating and planning control by the representatives of the whole people." Lassalle in the eighteen-
sixties hoped to convert Prussia into a democratic state
that would provide capital for the development of self-
governing producers in cooperative societies. Something
of this general theory seems to be on trial today in
Yugoslavia, where state-owned enterprises are managed
by workers' councils.

Lassalle's theories, widely accepted by German workers,
brought him into conflict with Marx and Engels and with
their theories of class struggle and of the state as agent
for the dominant class. Nevertheless, at the Congress of
Gotha (1875) there was a fusion of German Marxist and

Lassallian parties based on a program which Marx sharply criticized in one of his more important critical documents. It was a practical fusion which seemed necessary to withstand Bismarck's anti-socialist crusade. (In opposing socialism Bismarck pioneered in welfare measures appealing to workers.) Thus socialism brought into being the welfare state which tended to weaken its revolutionary appeal. The German socialists became theoretical Marxists who acted much like Lassallians. At the turn of the century, the powerful Social Democratic Party was greatly disturbed (but not split) by Eduard Bernstein's revisionism. He emphasized the probability of gradualist or evolutionary progress toward socialism, and lost out to the more orthodox Marxist, Kautsky. In 1914 he and Kautsky reunited as members of the anti-war minority of the Party. Neither side wanted a violent revolution; both sides were loyal Germans. Thus, the Party's actions during most of the 20th century suggested to outside observers that Lassalle or Bernstein had won, not the self-proclaimed Marxists. Yet the Party was nearer Marx than Lassalle in its close relations with labor unions.

The bitter clashes within the socialist and the radical labor union movements were between socialism and anarchism. These clashes were very often complicated, as in the case of Marx and Bakunin, by personal struggles for power. Anarchism, like socialism, is variable. Both systems have in common their opposition to the modern, nation-state's control over all its citizens and their institutions. Most—but not all—forms of anarchism were socialist in general theory and outlook, except in their attitude toward political action. Marx had predicted a withering away of the state after socialist victory. Ba-

kuninism was really a "sort of ultra leftist variant of
Marxism" which Max Nomad, following the Russian historian Stekhov, calls a forerunner of Lenin's Bolshevism.*

The loveliest and least immediately attainable version
of anarchism is Peter Kropotkin's Communist Anarchy,
but the most powerful expression of it before World War
I was anarcho-syndicalism. Most of this school emphasized such methods of class struggle as direct action,
sabotage, and general strike, and eschewed political action at the polls. The Socialist Labor Party in the U.S.,
whose outstanding leader was Daniel De Leon, held that
it should appeal to the electorate to vote for the abolition of the state. The Industrial Workers of the World,
(I.W.W.) once strong in the U.S., were also syndicalists,
though following a different pattern. Not much interested
in theory as such, the I.W.W. opposed political action,
i.e., voting, and put its trust in direct action. The syndicalists believed that the trade union (rather than the
older, anarchist "free group") should serve as the basis
of a free stateless society.

On the eve of World War I, socialists, as distinct from
anarchists and anarcho-syndicalists, had agreed essentially
to accept the state and its political action, although they
argued about the degree of emphasis on immediate demands and the pace of gradualism. Factually this argument was connected with the degree of democracy in a
state, the state's attitude to reforms, and the consequent
position of labor unions. The latter in most nations were
originally brought into being by radicals of a socialist per-

* See Nomad's excellent essay, "The Evolution of Anarchism and
Syndicalism, a critical view in European Ideologies," edited by Feliks
Gross.

suasion, but as they achieved strength, they became more
and more concerned with immediate benefits. They were
less revolutionary in outlook. It was not only preachers of
bliss in the hereafter who seemed to be talking of "pie in
the sky by and by" to the masses of workers who were
now concerned with bread, and maybe some cake. Nevertheless, the ideology of the largest continental European
labor unions before World War I was democratic socialist
however their relations to socialist political parties might
vary.

In most of Europe the relation between socialist parties
and trade unions was, and still is, close ideologically and
practically. The earliest unionism—the English—was originally militantly radical, if not dogmatically socialist. It
was subject to severe repression and was broken with the
collapse of Chartism. Following that defeat of the socialist
unions, the "New Model" unions arose. Philip Taft writes:

"The typical 'New Model' union, the Amalgamated Society
of Engineers, provided both strike benefits and insured its
members against unemployment, sickness and old age. In
contrast to the earlier unions, the Engineers, as did the unions
in other trades, relied on their own economic power which
was based on a monopoly of the labor supply."

Socialist agitation and education continued. In the
1880's the New Model theory and practice were under-
mined by the great influx of semi-skilled and unskilled
workers who couldn't easily monopolize their particular
contributions to the industries employing them. Then
began an infiltration of socialism into the British labor
movement. It was religious (mostly non-conformist),
ethical, and Fabian, rather than dogmatically Marxist.

The present Labor Party is the result; it is a socialist
party which is closely tied in organizationally with the
powerful labor union movement. At Party conventions,
union leaders cast their unions' bloc votes, and numer-
ically dominate the party.

European labor unionism, of any strength, dates back
only to the middle decades of the 19th century. Unionism
is younger than socialism. In some countries—Spain is
a notable example—the ideological influence of syndicalism early in this century was far stronger than in Britain,
the Scandinavian countries, Germany or France. But in
general, in the more or less democratic countries, the
unions accept the state and try to use political action as
well as collective bargaining to better their condition.

The strife between socialism and anarchism, together
with the Franco-Prussian War, were responsible for the
death of the First International, originally known as the
International Working Men's Association. Founded in
London in 1864, its headquarters were transferred to New
York, where it died in 1872. The Second International was
set up in 1889 and lasted until it was broken by World
War I. Though it was definitely socialist rather than
anarchist, its sessions reflected the many differences
among socialists. It was reorganized after its suspension
during World War II.

Socialist and labor-unionist activities in the U.S. roughly
paralleled European developments. The American environment was different from the European; the growth
of American socialism was less robust. (This will be
treated in a later chapter.)

Before the first world war it was anarchism rather than

socialism which was associated in fact, and still more in the popular mind, with violence including assassination as a legitimate form of direct action. There were, however, anarchists who renounced violence. They hated the political state in good measure because it used and bred violence. The majority of democratic socialists were not pacifist; in nations where they had the ballot, they usually disclaimed the use of violence, unless they thought it necessary in defending what they had legitimately won against an unscrupulous burgeois or capitalist opposition. They wholeheartedly supported strikes as relatively non-violent forms of the worker's struggle for justice.

In the early years of this century, syndicalism, repudiated by socialism, was associated not only with the general strike—its principal weapon—but with violence. This association was largely due to Georges Sorel's book, *Reflecting on Violence,* in which he praised syndicalism-with-violence. The book had a considerable vogue. Max Nomad says that it gave violence an importance which it did not have in the minds of the rank and file syndicalists. "Sorel," Nomad believes, "was at bottom a moralist. He saw in working class violence a means of disturbing the 'social peace' (which in his opinion was a corrupting influence both upon the workers and their capitalist masters; an influence which was bound to lead the world to decadence and barbarism. Application of violence would, in his view, reduce and discredit the influence of the parliamentary socialists who were trying to reconcile the working masses with the existing social order. It would also arouse the enthusiasm of the masses and thus lift the individual worker above the level of a purely animal existence. It would bring the element of beauty and heroism into his life. And, last but not least, it would serve as a healthy stimulus for the bourgeoisie."

It is significant that Georges Sorel left syndicalism for the pro-monarchists of Action Francaise who claimed on moral grounds to be opponents of bourgeois democracy. In a sense they were forerunners of fascism. Ultimately he and a great many of his former syndicalist comrades became Bolsheviks. Between fascists, Bolsheviks, and world wars, Sorel's praise of violence as a cleansing force was exposed as horrible absurdity.

Obviously this stark description of the origin and development of socialism up to this century is not a complete history. It is intended to give the necessary background for later appraisal of present-day socialism. I have always—even before becoming a socialist—appreciated socialism as a great and, on balance, liberating movement in social history, a movement possessed of a very lofty goal for mankind. I confess that its history contains chapters of dreary, ugly, factional strife. Many of the battling theorists were declassé middle-class intellectuals to whom modern psychological analysts would attribute personal motives other than (or in addition to) a love of the exploited masses.

But the Apostles of Revolution are not wholly to be explained psychologically in terms that would deny them credit for devoted concern for the working masses, so long exploited by one form or another of the master class. Most of them suffered for their beliefs.

It is, however, to the anonymous, devoted rank-and-file socialists in the years before the great wars, to whom my admiration goes out. Their steadfast devotion, their endurance, their willingness to sacrifice such little security as they might have had for a brighter day for their children is beyond praise. Socialism was their religion in the best sense of that word. They belong to the noble company of those of whom the world was not worthy.

IV.

Socialism and
Two World Wars

THE GREATEST VIOLENCE of our violent century has
not been associated with social revolution or risings of
the workers or struggles of colonial peoples to be free,
but with the power conflicts of nations and empires. We
must examine the role of socialism as it affected and was
affected by two world wars. Socialism could not avert,
or guide these wars.

Before 1914, socialism was making substantial progress
in many nations and in the development of internationalism, especially among workers. Its influence was becoming world-wide even among the slowly awakening colonial
peoples in Asia and in parts of Africa. Its internal conflicts
in the International did not split it, but revealed vigor of
thought and concern for real issues.

In Europe, the Russo-Japanese War marked the emergence in strength of the Japanese Empire at Russia's
expense, and was attended by popular rebellion against
the Tsar's autocracy. In that revolt the socialist-inspired

workers rather than the liberals or the peasants took the lead. All these social elements were involved, but co-operation was poor. Trotsky was president of the St. Petersburg Soviet. The government put down armed revolt by armed force and granted some very moderate reforms. The discussion in socialist ranks concerning the conditions for successful revolution, and the way revolutions should be understood and guided, brought Lenin and Trotsky—who did not then altogether agree—into general prominence. The socialists were divided into Bolsheviks and Mensheviks, but remained in the same party. The great conflict out of which communism was to come did not split the Socialist International which, however, had its distinct right and left wings.

The Socialist International concerned itself with the subject of war: the Boer and Russo-Japanese wars were but recently over and the political atmosphere was permeated by Franco-German hatred, Anglo-German naval competition and German militarism. At the Stuttgart International Conference in 1907, a long resolution was passed which considered the connection of war with capitalism, and the duty of workers and their parliamentary representatives to oppose armaments and money grants for war. It urged the substitution of national militias for standing armies. Finally it declared:

"'If a war threatens to break out, it is a duty of the working class in the countries affected, and a duty for their parliamentary representatives, with the aid of the International Bureau as an active and coordinating power, to make every effort to prevent the war by all means which seem to them the most appropriate—means which naturally vary according to the intensity of the class-struggle and to the political situation in general.

"'Should war none the less break out, it is their duty to intervene in order to bring it promptly to an end, and with all their strength to make use of the economic and political crisis created by the war to stir up the deepest strata of the people and precipitate the fall of capitalist domination.'"

Cole comments:

"Thus, in the final operative paragraphs the Russian Social Democrats got their way, and the parties of the International were formally pledged not merely to do their best to end it at once and to use the occasion for action to bring about the fall of capitalism. In the final resolution nothing was said about the general strike, or about insurrection—the Germans saw to that; but thanks to the Russian addition the prescription for action went a long way beyond the mere parliamentary protests which alone had been explicitly set forth in Bebel's draft. The general strike was not ruled out— it was passed over in silence; and the same can be said of insurrection, which can indeed be regarded as implicit in the final paragraph.

"The resolution, in its ultimate shape, seems to have satisfied everybody. Even Herve voted for it, leaping on a table to mark his enthusiasm. The delegates felt sure that they had done something almost heroic, while stopping short of incommoding the German comrades by any awkward references to insurrection that might have got them into trouble with the German Government." *

Nevertheless, this Stuttgart resolution proved a weak guide to socialist parties when the nations, walking in the path of capitalist imperialism, "stumbled and staggered" (in Lloyd George's words) into World War I. That was not a war to make the world safe for democracy and

* *The History of Socialist Thought* by G. D. H. Cole.

Wilson could not make it so. The minority socialists in Britain and Germany and the American Socialist Party were right in seeing it as power conflict between imperial systems in which capitalist profit was tied up. The secret treaties of the European allies, unknown to the peoples of the world until after the United States was in the war, proved this to the hilt. It was, as Major-General J. F. C. Fuller, the British military historian elaborated, stupid in its origin and more stupid and brutal in its blind continuance after the Germans were checked at the First Battle of the Marne. Everybody had something to win by a negotiated peace. The U.S. would never have joined had it been able to trade with both belligerents as it traded with the Allies. In short, the war was a colossal blunder, as well as a crime against humanity.

In retrospect, this conclusion seems logical. Some socialists saw it, and the socialist theory of war, with its passionate and deeply felt affirmations of the solidarity of the workers, should have led socialists into action. Admittedly action would have been difficult; a strike against mobilization would have been regarded as a seditious or revolutionary act. But socialists had discussed revolution on less serious provocation than a war—a war which would set workers to fighting workers in the name of governments to which they all professed deep ideological opposition. The workers on both sides were strongly organized into unions and socialist parties. A simultaneous strike in Germany, Austria-Hungary and France would have had the effect of gaining time for sober second-thought. The British, unlike the continentals, had no conscriptive power over civilians, but British socialists and labor unions could have helped check the headlong rush to war by instituting a general strike. So might have the Russians whose organized radical parties and labor unions, while not very strong, had by no means been wiped out by the defeat of the 1905 rising.

The very eloquent right wing French socialist, Jean Jaures, had talked strike should the danger of war arise. So had the Scotch socialist, Keir Hardie, leader of the Independent Labor Party. He thought that the labor movement could probably prevent war by threatening to strike or, if necessary, by striking. The great majority of socialists were as paralyzed as the rest of the European populace in this war of blundering imperialist governments. They also suffered more than they knew from the religion of nationalism. Very soon they were murdering each other just as docilely, if not as cheerfully, as Christians—with more experience behind them—were murdering Christians, and Jews were murdering Jews. The great gods of rival national sovereignties had spoken. Who would withstand them?

Thus socialists lost an opportunity unparalleled in history—an opportunity that could not come again. The circumstances under which Hitler later initiated the second world war were quite different. He had taken the precaution of crushing the German Social Democratic Party.

There were socialist minorities who steadfastly opposed the war. They gathered in two conferences, the first at Zimmerwald in Switzerland, the second at Kienthal. Lenin was a significant figure of both. His opposition to a war which he wished to turn into revolution proved a great asset to him in world opinion during the tumultuous postwar days. In a sense Zimmerwald and, more particularly, Kienthal were forerunners of the Third International.

While Lenin spoke primarily for those who wanted to turn war into revolution, others were primarily concerned to stop a war which they considered a crime against humanity. The difference in emphasis was an important factor in subsequent socialist thinking.

The American Party was an exception to the general rule that the majority of the democratic socialist parties found reason to support the war on one side or the other along with their fellow countrymen. In general, socialist efforts to bring it to some sort of end lacked power and imagination. Such efforts were, of course, limited to a great extent by laws and decrees against "sedition."

The American Party suffered from this governmental persecution as well as from the defection of a minority which included some of the Party's leaders. It is a temptation to insert a chapter on the crimes of the Wilson Administration and of other organized powers, especially the churches, against civil liberties during and after World War I. American public opinion as a whole was guilty. But for our present purpose only two observations are relevant. The first is that Wilson lost the socialist support he sorely needed for his League of Nations. The League, which could have been the beginning of an effective internationalism, was damned in American socialist minds because of its close association with the Peace of Versailles—a treaty which did so much to prepare the way for new wars. President Wilson's domestic policy, symbolized by the arrest and conviction of Gene Debs and the President's refusal to pardon him, cost Wilson further support.

Once, with a committee of the Civil Liberties Bureau (which Wilson refused to see), I warned his then chief advisor, Col. House, that the President was destroying the support which he had sought by his famous declaration of Fourteen Points because he consistently put the enemies of his liberalism into office and its friends (or potential friends) in jail. To no avail. Col. House thought that the administration could do without the help of civil libertarians and socialists.

My second comment on the first world war and the American Socialist Party is that I have never accepted the opinion, quite general among socialists, that persecution under Wilson was a major cause of the Party's decline: Debs, prisoner in the Atlanta Penitentiary, got 915,302 votes on the socialist ticket in 1920. Anti-war sentiment grew rapidly as the twenties advanced. I know, from my own experience, that the socialist war-stand ceased to be an obstacle, and in many quarters was a help, in getting a hearing, at least by the time of the La Follette campaign in 1924. The communist split had far more to do with socialist reverses.

Stamped indelibly upon my mind is the joy with which I welcomed the Armistice of November 11, 1918, and with it, a hope, amounting almost to conviction, that the world could not again rush into such an agony of folly and brutality. It was to democratic socialism that I looked for a peaceful revolutionary rebuilding of Europe. Instead, as all men know, we got communism, fascism and nazism. A child born on Armistice Day would not have quite reached his majority when World War II came upon us.

Democratic socialism was by no means utterly defeated in those years. It was a force in building up the welfare state. It was something of a bulwark in many nations against communist totalitarianism, and the latter's denial of individual freedom. Socialism in the broad sense of increase in public ownership and government planning, was necessarily stimulated by the war.

Woodrow Wilson's League of Nations will live in history (if mankind lives) as a pioneer in international organization advocating the substitution of law for war. But the League of Nations could not withstand the forces of vengeance and hate loosed upon mankind. Nor could it prevail against the religion of aggressive nationalism. I never thought that it could. Not even if the U.S. had joined it.

In 1920 the Socialist platform urged:

"The Government of the U.S. should initiate a movement to dissolve the mischievous organization called the 'League of Nations' and to create an international parliament, composed of democratically elected representatives of all nations of the world based upon the recognition of their equal rights, the principles of self-determination, the right to national existence of colonies, and other dependencies, freedom of international trade and trade routes by land and sea, and universal disarmament, and be charged with revising the Treaty of Peace on the principles of justice and conciliation."

While the majority of socialists had shared these sentiments, they modified their position in the light of world developments. In my first two presidential campaigns (1928 and 1932) we favored joining the League on conditions then easily obtainable. It was Roosevelt who, in the campaign of 1932, gave the final *coup de grace* to efforts to put the U.S.A. into the League of Nations. Earlier the Socialist Party had been outspoken in urging American acceptance of the World Court.

Democratic socialism in Europe grew within the limits

of national loyalties. It constituted the government of Britain even as a minority party under Ramsay Macdonald, who had opposed the war of 1914–18. In office, he deserted his party. The French party constituted the government of Leon Blum in 1936. Democratic socialists formed the largest single party in the short-lived republic in Spain. That legitimate republican government, hurt by Spanish factionalism, suffered military defeat by Franco, who was powerfully supported by Mussolini and Hitler. Stalin gave the Loyalists some support, but at a great price. For his efforts he received gold, and his agents were permitted to interfere in Spanish affairs while the democracies, the British, French and American governments, stood by enforcing a most unneutral "neutrality." This action, or inaction, was a great encouragement to Hitler in preparing for World War II, yet it had little effective opposition from the official European socialist parties; the British Labor Party switched—too late. The American Party favored active support of the republic—short of military intervention.

In other words, while democratic socialism made some gains, the parties of aggressive action were anti-democratic —fascist, nazi, and communist. The outstanding leaders were those evil men, Mussolini, Hitler, Stalin. The Iberian peninsula produced Salazar in Portugal and Franco in Spain. In Europe, before World War II, democratic socialism produced good men, but no correspondingly strong leaders. It was a failure shared with other democratic parties, with the important exceptions of Franklin Delano Roosevelt and Winston Churchill (a Conservative).

Perhaps one should add the name of Gandhi, whose theory and practice, so far as it could be put into conventional Western political terms, was democratic and agrarian socialist—but not Marxist. His great service to his country and to the world was in proving that nonviolent methods—at least under some circumstances—could be a positive force for revolutionary change. This gave some basis for hope of better things in a world apparently dedicated to faith in force, even in force raised to the nth power of violence by the development of nuclear power. (Yet, as we have noted, his people gave one of the saddest examples of popular violence at the time of the partition of India and Pakistan after the British Labor government —socialist—which came to power in 1945 had granted independence.)

The outstanding failure of socialism occurred in Germany in 1914 when socialism appeared to be at its strongest. It failed first of all because the majority of socialists accepted the Kaiser's war and further, because of socialism's failure to reorganize Germany after the war—a failure which culminated in socialism's crushing defeat by nazism. One could write sympathetically of the reasons for the failure and applaud some temporary successes. One could point out the role played by Stalinist communism, and the general cowardice of the bourgeois democratic parties before Hitler. But one is left with the fact that our great hope for socialism before 1914, and again after 1945, was not fulfilled. Was it socialism as socialism, or man as man, who failed?

The second world war had a moral quality which the first one lacked. It was a struggle against the demonic nazism obsessed by the ideal of Aryan (Germanic) supremacy. Victory in the second world war, more obviously than in the first, was a victory for democracy. But it was a victory sadly tainted by the terrible means employed to win it. It was compromised because one of the victors—Stalin—was almost as cruelly ruthless as Hitler.

Once more—and even more strikingly than in World War I—socialism, in the sense of social planning, increased welfare and economic activities of the national state, inevitably thrived, both in order to win the war and to rebuild Europe. The United Nations was more inclusive and vital than the defunct League of Nations. The United States was a member. It was, however, as ill equipped to perform its logically assigned tasks as was the League of Nations; its constitution was weak, and its component nations lacked a cooperative spirit.

The end of the old imperialisms rapidly brought independence to former colonies. The U.N. today has 110 member nations, but does not include the effective government of the most populous nation—China. In the emerging nations there is much devotion to Marxism, although its concepts are not completely understood. In many of these nations there is more socialism (as contrasted with laissez faire economy) than democracy. The indirect influence of socialism has been great, but organized democratic socialist parties have imperfectly met the challenge of the times.

The present International comprises 41 democratic socialist parties—one of them our American party. It recognizes five parties in exile. Affiliated with it, but not members of it, are the Asian Socialist Conference, the Socialist Union of Central-Eastern Europe, the International Union of Socialist Youth, and the International Union of Social Democratic Teachers.

Socialism has performed best in the Scandinavian countries, where socialist governments are usual. Tage Erlander has been premier of Sweden for eleven years; Sweden's social order, and the roles of parties, unions and cooperatives are much the same as they were before World War II, when Marquis Childs wrote his well known *Sweden: The Middle Way.*

I have praised the British Labor government for its work following the end of World War II. The socialist, Guy Mollet, Prime Minister of France, added no luster to socialism—especially in his wretched handling of Algeria. The German party, with exceptions, has been disappointing from 1914 on. It has now modified its old habit of professing Marxist fundamentalism, while practicing a not-very-radical reformism. Ernst Reuter, as mayor, did a magnificent job of rebuilding West Berlin.

In the appendix you will find the official statement of the International, which shows the basis of democratic socialist policy. In terms of the old disputes, it is parliamentary and gradualist, but still loyal to the old ideals. It has not succeeded in working out a strong, generally accepted policy for peace or in uniting its member parties on it.

In general the democratic socialist position will be better appreciated in its contrast with communism.

V.

Communism

COMMUNISM to the average American takes the place fundamentalist Christians assign to the devil. It is regarded, not as a system worthy of analysis, but rather as an object of total hate and rejection. Communism is never more dangerous than when it assumes the garb of an angel of light.

Communism, to its devoted adherents, and to millions of others, is the sole road to a utopia in which the state will have withered away. In it, men will be rewarded out of the general income, according to need, and will contribute to its production according to individual ability. Crime will disappear and each individual will realize the best of his efforts. The one enemy of mankind is capitalism and its offspring, capitalist imperialism.

But on the way to this utopia, communism, under Stalin, became the most absolute totalitarian government in history, which acted with a cruelty rivaling Hitler's. As the enemy of economic classes, it has created a new class of communist elite.

Communism believes that it offers the only correct interpretation and complete realization of Marxism, but it

64

has failed to come to power at the precise point which Marxist theory predicted: when capitalism had reached its peak, and presumably, had run its course. It has succeeded conspicuously in establishing its power in Russia and China, where capitalism was comparatively little developed and the economy predominantly agricultural.

Communism insists on monolithic unity of its followers, in theory and in action. Though it has used wholesale persecution to maintain unity, it is sharply divided in theory. This division brings the U.S.S.R. and China into open opposition, largely over issues of peace and methods of attaining individual freedom. Out of power, communists talk of civil liberty. In power they carry out, to a terrible extreme, the doctrine that the end justifies the means. They consider themselves justified in such distortions of truth and coercion of individuals and groups as may help them toward the desired end.

Although communism had its roots in left-wing socialism and native Russian extremism, it came to power less as the result of the new-found strength of the labor class than because of Russia's breakdown in the war and the ability of her revolution's leaders, Nicolai Lenin and Leon Trotsky. These paradoxes and the extraordinary phenomenon behind them need study and explanation.

At the end of World War I, Tsarist Russia lay in ruins, and it was questionable that it could be held together as a nation. By 1960, despite the suffering of World War II, Russia had become one of the world's two most powerful and vital nations: she had sent the first sputnik into space; she had put the first man into orbit—and had brought him safely back. She has accomplished all this under a system which her leaders call "socialism," a fact which once and for all removes socialism from the realm of utopian dreams.

What made possible this success of the Russian Social Revolution? Certainly not the original mass appeal of the tiny left-wing Bolshevik group. Certainly not the revolution's conformity to socialist expectations based on Marxist forecasts. Lenin himself did not expect his revolution to prevail unless it could spread, notably to Germany, where, by Marxist calculation, after Germany's defeat, it was surely due.

The answer, as we have suggested, is to be found first in the utter defeat of the Tsarist government in a war for which the masses—including most of the middle class and the peasants—had no responsibility and no conceivable interest except in a survival which their crushing defeat, despite their bravery in arms, made doubtful. The revolution was born of defeat in war.

Second was the extraordinary leadership of the small Bolshevik Party, or more accurately, of Lenin and Trotsky —especially the former. Nicolai Lenin was one of the few outstanding leaders of men of whom it may confidently be said that without them history would have been different. Had he died in Finland and before his final return to Russia, the Russian revolution, after some fashion, would probably have gone on; socialism would have been a great factor; and doubtless socialism would also have become much changed by it. But whatever the results, forty-five years later, we should have had neither the Russia nor the communism of the mid-century.

A third factor may well have been one quite contrary to the generally accepted Marxist theory that the industrial workers constituted the real revolutionary force. A great peasant country could somehow support life during all the

confusions of revolutionary change; a more highly industrial country might not have survived the general collapse
of its economic and social institutions. In Russia the workers, on the whole, came to the support of the Bolsheviks.
But in the civil war Lenin was able to secure in addition
the acquiescence of the peasants by supporting their de
facto appropriation of land. This was contrary to Bolshevik
theory and Stalin, after the peasants had helped Russia
to survive, returned ruthlessly to communizing the land.

A fourth factor of some importance was the verbal idealism of Bolshevism. (Its leaders might not like the word
idealism.) Here came a movement that was rooting out
the private capitalism which socialism had declared the
source of all ills. It was in earnest. Bolshevism was represented as the workers' party. (Actually few of its leaders
had a genuine working-class background, but the movement gave some workers a chance to rise in the hierarchy
of party and government.) Moreover communism's declared goals, doubtless sincerely held by many of its followers, were extremely high. Communists were working
for the fulfillment of the Marxist hope of a stateless, fraternal society. Just how this society would work neither
Marx nor Lenin ever made clear. Bellamy's *Looking Backward* was far more explicit.

It soon became painfully apparent that in communist
theory and practice this goal was remote in the Soviet
Union. The immediate fact was the dictatorship of the
proletariat, or, in reality, the dictatorship of the Communist Party. Since a party is too large for dictatorship it had
to be a dictatorship of a collective leadership, which, even
under Lenin, had become the dictatorship of a man. And
to Lenin, as Max Nomad says, "Everything was ethical

that helped the cause of Leninism."

But communists were not the only people to assume
that the end justifies the means or to ignore the bitter
truth that absolute power corrupts absolutely: in spite of
the mounting evidence of this truth, Bolshevism was
doubtless helped internally, as certainly it was helped
abroad, by the approval of millions of workers and their
sympathizers, because in the assertion of Bolshevik power
the mighty were put down and those of low degree exalted.
Men are so made as to find compensation for many hard-
ships in the turn of fortune's wheel.

The situation in which the Bolsheviks achieved power
was chaotic. Bolshevik success in part was due to success
not only in seizure of land, but at first in the taking over of
factories by the workers. The new government, even in the
midst of civil war against its opponents and their foreign
allies was able to take over the factories—nominally in the
name of the working class—but, to quote Max Nomad, "In
industry, as in the army, the Bolshevik intellectuals and
'class conscious' *ex-workers* were the commanding officers
while the workers remained obedient privates."

Bolshevik success in Russia seemed so contrary to Marx's
opinion that "no social formation ever disappears before
all the productive forces are developed for which it has
room" (*Preface to Critique of Political Economy*) that
Lenin and Trotsky believed at first that the success of their
revolution depended upon its igniting revolution in Western lands—notably Germany—which, they thought, were
ready for it under the Marxist formula. But as everybody
knows the fires lighted by the communist revolution in the
West were extinguished or brought under control. In
France and Italy, for instance, the Party is strong, but op-

erates today within a democratic framework of elections.

In truth Marx had left little theoretical guidance to the able Russians who operated as his most orthodox disciples. Lenin made his own Marxism as he went along, a fact his democratic socialist critics pointed out in challenging his claim to be the one infallible interpreter of the Master. Lenin's skillful pragmatism allowed him successfully to operate under the mantle of orthodox Marxism; this was especially valuable to him in forming his own Socialist International.

Early in 1921 the Bolshevik government, victor over its various enemies in arms, was confronted by the mutiny of some of its bravest and most loyal supporters—the sailors of Kronstadt. They were ruthlessly crushed, but their demand for a free market for peasants' crops was granted under the New Economic Policy which allowed the peasants free disposal of their produce after paying part of their crop as a grain tax. The government kept full control of the key industries, the banks and the transportation system, but considerable private enterprise was re-established in retail trade, home crafts and small workshops.

How long Lenin would have kept NEP had he lived, and how he would have ended it, we don't know. We know what Stalin did. In the years, 1928 to 1932, with inexorable cruelty, he enforced a collectivization of land at a cost of some four million peasant lives. The New Economic Policy died in governmental violence against which there was no organized violent revolt.

Unquestionably the masses benefited by the economics of the NEP. But in view of subsequent developments and the present economic conditions in Russia, I should again agree with Max Nomad who wrote that NEP succeeded temporarily "not because a free market is necessarily always more efficient than one controlled by the government, but because those in charge of management, procurement and distribution were (before NEP) in most cases amateurs, semi-educated ex-soapboxers skillful in quoting or misquoting Marx and Lenin, but inexperienced in any sort of practical work." It takes time, he says, to develop efficient management. To which I would add that efficient farm management, accepted more or less docilely by the collectivized workers, has apparently not yet arisen in the Soviet Union, and certainly not in China. Communism has yet to come up with a successful agricultural program.

Once in political power, Lenin's version of socialism no more brought about brotherhood on earth than did official Christianity. From the beginning, social democrats were suppressed as heretics, and under Stalin, the communist revolution devoured its own children on a scale without precedent. On this subject the harshest criticisms of outsiders were confirmed by Khrushchev in his famous speech on Stalin's criminal "cult of personality."

But that denunciation never included Stalin's crimes against non-communists, including democratic socialists. During his detestable alliance with Hitler at the beginning of World War II, Stalin was responsible for the massacre of Polish officers in the Katyn forest, the wholesale evacuation of Polish socialists into horrible labor camps, and the murder of the great Polish-Jewish socialist leaders, Ehrlich and Alter, who—after Hitler's attack had forced Russia into war—forgave Stalin his crimes against Poland and themselves and supported the war. Finally Stalin refused to come to the relief of Warsaw during its gallant ris-

ing. This was part of his deliberate plan to weaken social
democrats, and thus to facilitate the seizure of Poland at
war's end.*

Outwardly, communism under Stalin began to prosper.
Stalin, toward the end of 1934, at long last aware of Nazi
power, rather successfully went in for a "united front."
It was a united front in which Social Democrats were to
play the role of the "Young Lady from Niger, who went
for a ride on a tiger./ They came back from the ride/ With
the lady inside/ and the smile on the face of the tiger."

A foreign communist, who called himself J. Peters and
who served as a kind of commissar to America, wrote a
manual for the American Party which proclaimed the
Party "the general staff of the proletariat." It contained in-
structions for manipulating the United Front as a communist tool. I, having always on principle defended civil
liberty for communists (I opposed the Smith and Mc-
Carran Acts), can testify from experience about communist intolerance. For example, I remember how in 1934
communists violently broke up a great socialist and labor
mass meeting in Madison Square Garden, which had been
called to protest Dollfuss' crimes against Viennese workers. During my presidential campaign of 1944 when World
War II made communists temporarily ultra American
patriots, the *Communist Daily Worker* urged the government to suppress my speaking because of my concern over
the approach to peace. Their Western organ, the *People's
World*, appealed unsuccessfully for a mob to break up my

* It was Oscar Lange, the noted economist, then an American citizen,
who first told me that this was a deliberate policy to make sure of communist control of Poland. He said that he saw nothing to do but accept
it. After the war, he abandoned American citizenship and returned to his
native land in which he has held important posts.

meeting in Seattle. The story of the price they exacted from the Spanish Loyalists in the Spanish Civil War has often been told, notably by George Orwell in *Homage to Catalonia*.

Mrs. Thomas and I were in Russia in 1937 when Stalin favored the united front and wanted the *valuta* of tourism. We were first refused visas, apparently because I had been a member of Dr. John Dewey's Committee for Justice to Trotsky—something which the latter did not practice in relation to the American Socialist Party. We were granted visas after an interview with Ambassador Troyanovsky, who expressed the hope that on my return I would support a Committee for Justice to the Soviet Union. Although definitely non-communist, I was very anxious to see the Soviet venture at its best.

On the whole our visit was a melancholy experience. It occurred during an interval in the ghastly purge trials. Russians were afraid to be seen with Americans. A young American from our embassy, who spoke Russian, took me to call on his landlady. Near the entrance to the apartment house we met the house chairman who seemed so suspicious of us that my friend decided that our visit might jeopardize his landlady's standing. (Later he left the Soviet Union a heartbroken man because of the sudden and complete disappearance of his fiancée, a beautiful Russian girl. He resigned his post, came out through Siberia, attempted—at some danger to himself—to get news of her. His efforts were in vain.)

Even then I was favorably impressed by communist efforts to conquer illiteracy and generally to improve education—but by very little else. We were grateful to our guide, an extremely friendly young girl, who seemed very sincere. We had paid in advance for a few days' service, but the government saw to it that she met us at the Polish border and stayed with us until our train pulled out at the Finnish border.

Consumer goods were scarce and inferior; the pretentious new buildings shoddy. The differences in the rate of pay for various types of labor were proportionately as great as in the U.S., and there was no sign of individual freedom. The prison workcamps were crowded with millions, whose offences had not been proved in proper proceedings. Some of them I saw working under armed guard on a development project. The horror of these camps has been vividly described in *One Day in the Life of Ivan Denisovich.*

On our last night in Moscow, thanks to Major Famonville of our embassy staff, several of us Americans and the Major got front row seats for the ballet, *The Flames of Paris,* at the Moscow Opera House. That night Stalin also attended the ballet. He arrived late, but we waited for him. He tried never to show himself to his supposedly adoring public. As was customary, the ballet members who were not performing were crowded into the box opposite his. Throughout the entire performance they stared at the dictator as though hypnotized. He left the instant the final curtain fell.

Before the ballet began, a Russian officer, obviously of high rank, stood up in his box above Stalin's and appeared to be looking over the house. Our escort was sure he was doing just that, and identified him as General Friedman—I think I remember the name correctly. It seems that our escort and Friedman had both been young officers in Eastern Siberia after World War I when both Russians and

Americans were somewhat united in concern over the
presence of the Japanese. "But now," our escort said, "he's
too high up. He is a great friend of Stalin's." A few days
later we read a brief announcement of Friedman's arrest,
along with Marshal Tukachevsky. Not many weeks later,
as we left Paris for home, the papers announced his liqui-
dation. This was the climax of my Russian impressions
which were more than confirmed by Stalin's alliance with
Hitler. That alliance was broken by Hitler, not Stalin. Not
even the Russians' defense of their country against the
German monster could remove my horror of Stalin's totalitarianism.

It is not surprising, then, that when I read George Orwell's *1984* I was ready to accept it as realistic prophecy
rather than satire. Had anyone then described the U.S.S.R.
as it is today, or as Khrushchev wants it to be in 1980
(when he thinks real communism can begin), I should
have thought him mad. I do not so much refer to Russia's
obvious military strength, or to her pioneering achievements in space, as to the apparent attitude and optimism
of her people, their achievements in science, music, sports,
yes, and literature. It is a wonderful people which has survived two German invasions within less than 30 years, a
cruel civil war, Stalin's brutal despotism, his slave labor
camps, and his wholesale executions of natural leaders.

The Russia which has thus survived has done so under
the communist version of socialism. It could scarcely have
done so if communism were merely evil incarnate in its
polity and culture. Despite its crimes, the communist revolution cannot be so easily dismissed. It has proved capable
of some degree of evolution and it becomes important to
ask in what direction that evolution is tending: not in the

direction of *1984* but rather in a slow reverse. Khrushchev
was Stalin's man and acted as such until the latter's death.
Hitler's only rival at coldblooded murder for personal
power was Stalin. But by 1962 there were changes, evi-
denced by the new communist attack on the cult of personality, vividly symbolized by the removal of Stalin's
body from its place in the tomb beside Lenin (still honored
by millions of the devout). Even more important is the
turn Russian communism has taken toward decentralization.

Theoretically this is embodied in the New Program of
the Soviet Communist Party, adopted in 1961. That Program, written around 1960, claims that at the end of 20
years, the material and technical basis of communism will
have been laid. Then the communist order, to which the
present socialist order is an approach, can begin. The Program must be taken as the official interpretation of communist doctrine as the dominant communists in the strongest communist-controlled nation conceive it. (Just how far
Yugoslavia's Tito on the right and, more especially, China's
Mao Tse-tung on the left, would disagree is another matter.
Competent observers warn us that Stalinism is by no
means dead, even in the U.S.S.R.)

Stripped of the usual communist rhetoric the new program for the next twenty years calls for the steady development of what we would call a welfare state. Thus Harri-
son E. Salisbury describes this phase of the program:

"Large segments of the social goals of the program have
been lifted bodily from the welfare state plans long advocated by the British Labor Party, the Scandinavian Socialist
Parties and the Social Democratic Party of Germany.
"Not a few of the provisions which Mr. Krushchev's pro-

gram hopes to achieve after a decade or two were enacted
into law in the United States under Franklin D. Roosevelt's
New Deal. Other provisos such as free midday meals in school
have long been in effect in the United States. Free midday
meals in factories are envisaged as a *crowning achievement
of Communism*. Actually, they have been provided by a
number of enterprising American capitalists for some time.

"Almost all of the social welfare goals specified in the
Communist Program are already the law of the land in one
western nation or another. Australia and New Zealand provide substantially more complete social legislation than the
Moscow plan.

"Two Soviet proposals are more 'original.' These are free
urban transit and free rent. Soviet rent, however, already is
so heavily state subsidized that it constitutes only about five
per cent of the average family budget. Possibly because of
this low cost Soviet housing—except for new construction of
the past two or three years—has been notably deficient in
area, maintenance and convenience. The goal of free municipal transport sounds vaguely reminiscent of New York
City's famous 'five-cent subway fare'—long maintained
despite its uneconomic nature as a sop to voters.

"The other 'Communist' goals, such as more private automobiles, an extensive network of highways, better shopping
facilities, and the like, are lifted directly from the life of
prosperous western nations like the United States." *

To this sort of criticism Mr. Khrushchev's program in
effect replies by arguing that welfare programs in capitalist countries were prompted by fear of the rising power
of labor, that they coexist with great extremes of poverty
and wealth, and much unemployment, and that they are

---

* In his introduction to *Khrushchev's "Mein Kampf"* (Belmont Press).
The book contains the full program plus the introduction under the pub-
lisher's misleading description, "The Threatening Prelude to World
War III."

generally insecure. Capitalist nations promise no such rate
of progress in the production as Khrushchev promises
within the next 20 years, daring at the same time to give
some fairly definite statistical estimates for both industry
and agriculture. Thus:

"Within 20 years metallurgy will develop sufficiently to
produce about 250,000 million metric tons of steel a year."
"Productivity of labor in agriculture will rise not less than
150 per cent in 10 years and five to six fold in 20 years."
And then the communist society can begin.

The program ignores one fact which is bothersome to
all socialist theorists: while Russia's annual rate of increase
of production is great—greater at present than America's
—it is less than that of two other countries which suffered
greatly in war, West Germany and Japan, and whose economies, though mixed, are predominantly capitalist.

There are, I think, certain changes in communist dogma
embodied in the program which are more important than
American anti-communists realize. It renounces the inevi-
tability of war so long as capitalism exists, and admits that
violent revolution may not be required to establish communism. While the program contains the usual communist
denunciation of social democratic parties, it advocates cooperation with them wherever possible. (This may be a
mere renewal of the insincere united front policy of the
thirties.) It admits some possibility of buying out capitalist
monopolies. I quote certain passages, first on buying out
the bourgeoisie:

> "It may well be that as the forces of Socialism grow, the
> working-class movement gains strength and the positions of
> capitalism are weakened, there will arise in certain countries
> a situation in which it will be preferable for the bourgeoisie,

as Marx and Lenin foresaw it, to agree to the means of production being purchased from it and for the proletariat to 'pay off' the bourgeoisie.

"The success of the struggle which the working class wages for the victory of the revolution will depend on how well the working class and its party master the use of all forms of struggle—peaceful and non-peaceful, parliamentary and extra-parliamentary—and how well they are prepared to replace one form of struggle by another as quickly and unexpectedly as possible."

Next, on cooperation with social democrats:

"Overcoming the split in its ranks is an important condition for the working class to fulfill its historic mission. No bastion of imperialism can withstand a closely knit working class that exercises unity of action. The Communist Parties favor cooperation with the Social Democratic Parties not only in the struggle for peace, for better living conditions for the working people and for the preservation and extension of their democratic rights and freedoms, but also in the struggle to win power and build a Socialist society.

"At the same time Communists criticize the ideological positions and Right-opportunist practice of social-democracy and expose the Right Social-Democratic leaders, who have sided openly with the bourgeoisie and renounced the traditional Socialist demands of the working class."

And, most important of all, on war:

"It is possible to avert a world war by the combined efforts of the mighty Socialist camp, the peace-loving non-Socialist countries, the international working class and all the forces championing peace. The growing superiority of the Socialist forces over the forces of imperialism, of the forces of peace over those of war, will make it actually possible to banish world war from the life of society even before the complete victory of socialism on earth, with capitalism surviving in a part of the world. The victory of Socialism throughout the world will do away completely with the social and national causes of all wars. To abolish war and establish everlasting peace on earth is a historical mission of Communism.

"General and complete disarmament under strict international control is a radical way of guaranteeing a durable peace. Imperialism has imposed an unprecedented burden of armaments on the people. Socialism sees its duty towards mankind in delivering it from this absurd waste of national wealth. The solution of this problem would have historical significance for mankind. By an active and determined effort the peoples can and must force the imperialists into disarmament.

"Socialism has offered mankind the only reasonable principle of maintaining relations between states at a time when the world is divided into two systems—the principles of the peaceful coexistence of states with different social systems, put forward by Lenin.

"Peaceful coexistence of the Socialist and capitalist countries is an objective necessity for the development of human society. War cannot and must not serve as a means of settling international disputes. Peaceful coexistence or disastrous war—such is the alternative offered by history. Should the imperialist aggressors nevertheless venture to start a new world war, the peoples will no longer tolerate a system which drags them into devastating wars. They will sweep imperialism away and bury it."

But Khrushchev, like Kennedy, wants disarmament derived from strength, not from weakness, and says so in no uncertain terms in paragraphs entitled, "The Strengthening of the Armed Forces and the Defence Potential of the Soviet Union," rather curiously "shoehorned," to use Mr. Salisbury's word, into the section on "The Tasks of the Party in the Spheres of State Development and the Further Promotion of Socialist Democracy."

The doctrine is that "as long as imperialism survives, the threat of aggressive wars will remain . . . In terms of internal conditions the Soviet Union needs no army." (Of course, in Khrushchev's book, Russia's relations with East Germany, Estonia, Latvia, Lithuania, Poland, Hungary, Czechoslovakia, Bulgaria and Rumania have nothing to do with imperialism. The section was written or adopted not long before communist rulers found that under communist emancipation from imperialism it was necessary to build that wall in Berlin to keep the emancipated in. Cooperation with social democrats has not included Willy Brandt, the Mayor of West Berlin.)

The section justifying Russian militarism follows sections giving the interesting news that the dictatorship of the proletariat has done its work in the U.S.S.R. The socialist state on the way to the communist goal

"has begun to grow over into a nation-wide organization of the working people of Socialist society. Proletarian democracy is becoming more and more a Socialist democracy of the people as a whole. The working class is the only class in history that does not aim to perpetuate its power. Having brought about a complete and final victory of socialism— the first phase of communism—and the transition of society to the fullscale construction of communism, the dictatorship of the proletariat has fulfilled its historic mission and has ceased to be indispensable in the USSR from the point of view of the tasks of internal development.

"The state, which arose as a state of the dictatorship of the proletariat, has become a state of the entire people, an organ expressing the interests and will of the people as a whole. Since the working class is the foremost and best organized force of Soviet society, it plays a leading role also in the period of the full scale construction of Communism. The working class will have completed its function of leader of society after Communism is built and classes disappear. . . .

"As Socialist democracy develops, the organs of state power will gradually be transformed into organs of public self-government. The Leninist principle of democratic centralism which insures the proper combination of centralized leadership with the maximum encouragement of local initiative, the extension of the rights of the union republics and greater creative activity of the masses, will be promoted. It is essential to strengthen discipline, control the activities of all the elements of the administrative apparatus, check the execution of the decisions and laws of the Soviet state and heighten the responsibility of every official for the strict and timely implementation of these laws."

Some rather specific emphasis follows concerning the increasing role of social organizations while full-scale construction of communism is in progress. By the time "the period of full-scale Communist construction is reached," when the coercive state has withered away, the Communist Party will be even more important than it is now as "the leading and guiding force of Soviet Society." Rigid rules insure "the Socialist principle of collective leadership." They call for the regular replacement in certain specified proportions, of all the members of elected bodies, ranging from primary organizations to the Central Committee, and at the same time for the preservation of continuity of leadership.

This whole section is worth studying as an ideal one-party society in which the State—at least in semantic terms—has withered, or is withering, away. The Party outlasts the State! There is no clear suggestion of tolerance of a rival party, but the one-party is to be democratized rather completely in structure. One may be permitted several grains of salt when recalling that at the time of its adoption the present Soviet constitution under which Stalin operated was hailed as a long step toward democracy. Whatever the program promises, Russia is today still a totalitarian state where whatever freedom writers and others enjoy is regarded as a concession rather than a right.

Nevertheless there has been a decided increase in tolerance of artists and writers. Khrushchev did not extend his vocal condemnation of abstract art to its prohibition. (His sentiment ought to help abstract art in the U.S.A. where many are convinced that Khrushchev is always wrong.) In economic matters there has been under Khrushchev considerable tolerance of decentralization of control over industry. He himself is a dictator of a decidedly different type, and less personally powerful than his old master, Stalin, whom he has denounced for the cult of personality. He has opponents in his own Party who are allowed to live.

I have had the privilege of reading in manuscript form, Alfred M. Bingham's account of Soviet experiments in democracy. His Russian is adequate, and he is now reporting on his third trip to Russia with his wife. They inquired especially into democratic developments by interviews with local leaders in the fields of law and education. Mr. Bingham's report seems to show some growth of what we should call democratization. He writes concerning elections: "Free elections in our sense are nowhere in sight in the Communist future. At the same time the people are getting more to say in the selection of their 'representatives' and more of them are being selected."

Mr. Bingham also reports some progress in popular participation by local Soviets in fulfillment of the Communist Program's aspiration that "fresh millions of working people may learn to govern the state." However, it seemed clear "that the activities of the volunteer participants in local government are less spontaneous than promoted from the top."

In discussing law and order as they exist under the Soviet machinery of peoples courts, Mr. Bingham reports that his recent discussions and observations of trials "merely confirm my earlier impressions; the rights of those accused of crimes are probably as secure, and the regular courts probably function as independently and conscientiously as in any Western country." His informants assured him that crime and juvenile delinquency were being *reduced*—rather a different view than the old communist contention that crime would *disappear* with the capitalist system.

Actually, in recent months, the authorities have instituted a kind of crusade to punish appropriation of state property—by blackmarketing, for example. For some such crimes the state is reinstituting capital punishment which, nominally, had been abolished in ordinary criminal procedures. A high percentage of Jews is to be found among those executed, which, as well as some other facts, suggests that anti-semitism is by no means wholly dead in Soviet society despite the government's boast of the number of Jews in high positions.*

* However, in the *New York Times*, July 20, 1962, Boris Nikiforov, Head, Criminal Law Department, U.S.S.R. Institute of Jurisprudence, answers an earlier letter in the *Times* from certain American clergymen, Catholic, Jewish and Protestant, by explaining that the "death sentence is passed only under aggravating circumstances." He gives no examples.

To go back to Mr. Bingham's report. It is generally believed that "with the increase of popular participation the role of courts and lawyers is expected to decline." At least one lawyer told him that when the utopian goals of communist society had been realized there would be no need for courts and lawyers—the old dream projected into an indefinite future. On the way to that future, says the Program, "the transition to communism means the extension of personal freedom and the rights of Soviet citizens." But only for right-thinking citizens. Mr. Bingham comments, "The notion that not only the minds of children but adults, too, must be protected from demoralizing influence seems a Soviet axiom." A paramount task, according to the Program, is the complete elimination of "survivals of bourgeois views and morals" and "remnants of private owner psychology."

This may be the ideal of the communist system, but practically, the communist government permits much personal property. Such things as private houses, estates, automobiles, and large cash savings are somehow classed as "articles of consumption," which articles Marx and Lenin permitted privately to be owned. There are great inequalities of wages. In Russia, direct income taxes are on their way to abolition but the tax system, or its equivalent, is very regressive. In 1962 Khrushchev felt obliged to increase the price of meat and butter: a very inefficient way of raising public revenue. Apparently there is very general

He concludes his letter thus: "Whoever appropriates the state or public property encroaches on the basic principles of life of Soviet society, hence on the basic principles of life of every Soviet man. That is why the Constitution of the U.S.S.R. says that Socialist property is sacred and inviolable." I recommend on this subject Moshe Decter's careful study *The Status of Jews in the Soviet Union* in *Foreign Affairs*, January, 1963.

employment and there seems to have been an abolition of the horrible slave work camps into which Stalin threw millions of his subjects for various alleged political heresies.

The market system is based on the use of money. Material incentives are openly used allegedly to increase production. There is no stockmarket and no living on dividends, but citizens may in accordance with the law inherit and bequeath property, and hold author's rights on scientific, literary and artistic works, inventions and discoveries. The prohibition against possession of more than one dwelling house seems to be violated by the Soviet ruling class, whose members usually have town and country houses. The pressure for more and better consumer goods seems evident and may be a strong reason for Khrushchev's interest in disarmament. There is plenty of other work for Russians to do.

What is particularly interesting is that it has been found necessary to allow the peasants, organized in kolkhozes and on state-owned farms, to own subsidiary plots of land, flocks, cattle, fowl and small agricultural equipment. Limits are put on such ownership. George Weller, veteran American journalist, after spending much time in rural areas, told me how striking was the higher degree of work and of corresponding results on the privately owned small plots as opposed to the large collectives where the workers are employed under management more or less as in factories. He told about a talk he had with a manager of one of these collectives who admitted getting a much larger wage than the workers. He also said, "But you needn't be sorry for the workers. Be sorry for me. I have to spend so much time on paper work that I haven't time to till my private plot as they do. That makes up the difference."

Since Stalin's time the state has undoubtedly relaxed its control over science, the arts and literature. But there is a long way to go. In the *Reporter*, March 15, 1962, Peter Viereck wrote at some length on the new "conspiracy of feelings against robotism" in the field of literature. There he found a "split personality." He reports concerning his Russian writer friends: "All writers I talked to stayed within 'correct' official lines as expected under a dictatorship. But they understand communism in very different ways." By and large, he continues, they are separated into two opposed camps, one still favoring Stalinism, if not Stalin himself, and the other much freer. The poet, Yevtushenko, whose work has attracted interest in England and America, belongs to the latter school. Viereck heard Yevtushenko read in Moscow and he writes: "The whole evening of poetry reading provided my most memorable personal impression of contemporary Soviet youth; its passion for the arts, its passion for liberty and racial tolerance. There all around me was the Russia I had learned to love, the Russia of generous ethical and aesthetic commitments. It was the young Russia that cheered, cried and laughed out of a natural, unaffected enthusiasm for free poetic self-expression, bursting forth far beyond the intentions of the government's current half-hearted, half-thaw." (A recent report by Brooks Atkinson confirms Mr. Viereck's account of Russian interest in poetry and the arts; the immense vitality of Moscow and the good quality and cheapness in price of its new housing—a great improvement over its earlier efforts in this field.)

The more I read and hear about the Soviet Union today, the more I marvel that it has come as far as it has, considering the terrible tyranny of Stalin from which so many families personally suffered. It was perhaps the war with all its suffering but with its victory over the Germans, crueler even than Stalin, which built up the national morale by a sense of pride in their triumph over what they had endured.

In spite of progress, I am still impressed by how far the Soviet needs to go to catch up with the West in material prosperity and in many of the freedoms (which we talk about, but do not ourselves value and conserve as we ought).

I believe that communism, as the official creed in the Soviet union and its satellites, will not be overthrown, but is being modified greatly by evolution. Its self-proclaimed goals, so contrary to Stalin's practice, remain very lofty.

I can claim no expert knowledge, but I am one of those who believe that *if* we avoid war, and *if* the present drift continues much as it is both in the U.S.S.R. and U.S.A., in a generation or so the actual differences between us will be slight. Most descriptions of modern Russia impress me by the similarities they reveal between the Russian people and ourselves. More and more I think that the contest between us will become primarily a contest of power rather than a true ideological struggle. Both sides will rationalize it semantically in terms of opposing ideologies (which will be even more imperfectly practiced than today). In reality, both will be garrison states—the U.S. probably with a larger element of individual rights.

VI.

Communism
in the World

JOHN REED'S FAMOUS BOOK title was prophetic. The ten days, in which Lenin came to power, truly shook the world. Communism is a missionary religion; its goal is a communist world; it is bothered by few scruples concerning the tactics used to advance its ideology and its power.

Until World War II, communism as a ruling power was confined to the Soviet Union that emerged from Tsarist Russia. It had, however, already become a great internal force in most of the world. By the time of the Potsdam agreements, Stalin had enlarged his borders directly at the expense of Poland and Finland, had absorbed Lithuania, Latvia, and Estonia (whose independence Lenin had recognized), and had become de facto overlord of the satellite states of Bulgaria, Rumania, Albania, Hungary, Yugoslavia, Poland, and—after a few years—East Germany. A minority Communist Party, under shadow of Russian military might, added democratic Czechoslovakia to the list in 1948.

This extension of communist power was due less to native parties strongly tied to Russian leadership than to the Russian military victory over Germany, which was greatly facilitated by non-communist Britain and America. What might have been, had the U.S.A. and Britain created a better peace plan, no one can positively affirm. Roosevelt's emphasis on the negative policy of proclaiming as the great war aim Germany's unconditional surrender, respect for Russia's contribution to allied victory over Hitler, coupled with an exaggerated fear that Stalin, crossed, might again make a separate peace with Hitler, made it easy for the communist dictator to take almost whatever he wanted in Europe. It even put Berlin a hundred miles within Russian-occupied territory.

The failure of the English-speaking powers to plan for genuine democratic independence of Eastern European nations, or to aid them as once they might have, was paralleled by their failure to promise anything in the East but destruction of the Japanese empire, independence of Korea—for which no preparations were made—and a return of Formosa to China without consulting Formosa. To this day no one knows why Berlin was left in a Russian zone, or why Korea was divided at the 40th parallel and its northern half handed over to Russian occupation. Against this whole approach to peace we American socialists earnestly protested. We wanted genuine independence in Eastern Europe and a plan for the independence of Western European colonies in Asia, similar to the plan arranged for the Philippines. Our voices aroused little attention in the campaign of 1944 and afterwards.*

* Our 1944 platform and subsequent statements are logically consistent with our 1962 platform on foreign policy. See Appendix II. Facts as they

That communism was not, and did not become, the free choice of Eastern European peoples under it, has been sorrowfully proved by history in Poland, Hungary and East Germany. It takes a wall in Berlin, guarded by soldiers, to hold in denizens of the East German "socialist" paradise.

In 1948, under Marshal Tito, Yugoslavia dared to break away from Stalin's overlordship and developed an interesting right wing communism under which workers' councils have greater control over industry than in the U.S.S.R. In 1963 Khrushchev seems to have healed this bitter breach —settling for more than mere coexistence, but less than Tito's absolute submission—in his effort to assert Russian leadership against the Chinese in the communist world.

In Milovan Djilas, author of *The New Class*, Yugoslavia has produced one of communism's most articulate critics. He was once very high in the governing elite. That he should again be in jail, this time for writing his *Conversations with Stalin*, is a fact more eloquent of what is wrong with communism than anything he has said about it. Not content with jailing his old friend and close comrade, Tito has warned Yugoslav writers thus: "We certainly did not want to teach writers and tell them what they must write but we do not allow anyone to write nonsense and caricature and distort our social life."

Communism's greatest victory since the war has not been in Europe—indeed it has lost ground in Western Europe—but in China, where it was carried to victory by Mao and his devoted partisans, without much help from

are can't be altered for the better by thermonuclear war to which alternatives must be found.

Stalin. It was a notable victory won by a comparative
handful of determined men who successfully exploited
both the general grievances of the people against Chiang
Kai-shek's weak and corrupt government, and the deep
desire of the peasants for land of their own. (In Hong
Kong in 1952, I listened to the members of an ardent anti-
communist "freedom front" who were almost as bitter in
their contempt for the old government as they were in
their hatred of the oppressive measures of the new masters
who were imposing a communist unity on their fatherland.
One of the ablest Far Eastern correspondents told me that
he had seen far more guns of American than of Russian and
Czech manufacture in use by Ho Chi Min's communists
fighting the French in Indochina. Chiang's corrupt generals had sold them.) Once more, even more conspicuously than in Russia, a social revolution succeeded which
did not follow the Marxist prescription for socialist progress.

China's revolution was certainly not primarily a revolution of an industrial working class. It was astonishingly
successful in building Chinese military strength—witness
the Korean war—and in promoting sanitation, education
and industry—all at a high price to individual freedom.
Communism, as I found in my travels in the fifties, became
a *mystique* of great power in Asia. Had it not worked
miracles, first in a broken Russia and then in China?

The Chinese Communists, under Mao Tse-tung, were
successful in improvising small scale industrial production
in the villages, before they acquired control of any large
urban centers. This, G. F. Hudson thinks, "certainly remained in their memories and was destined to play its part

in the Party's decision to adopt the commune system in 1958"—decision which they later modified. Mr. Hudson continues:

"The Chinese communes differ from Soviet collective farms in four ways. In the first place, they are bigger units in terms of membership. Secondly, they carry on industrial as well as agricultural production. Thirdly, they are organized—though this varies greatly from one commune to another—much more on a basis of 'collective living' than the Soviet kolkhoz. Fourthly, they are not only economic, but also military units, as the Soviet collective farms are not.

"The difference in size would not be by itself of great importance apart from inclusion of industrial enterprises. In the Soviet Union also there has been a tendency to amalgamate collective farms so as to form larger units, and the total number has been drastically reduced over the past twenty-five years. The amalgamations, however, have not altered the essentially agricultural character of the Soviet collectives, and the reason appears to have been mainly administrative convenience. In China, on the other hand, the idea of having economic units which can combine agriculture with industrial enterprises has certainly been the main reason for the replacement of groups of collective farms by units which may contain anything up to 20,000 households." *

In *The Other Side of the River, Red China Today*, Edgar Snow, a long-standing and exceedingly well-informed friend of communist leaders, tells us that, "all the nation's 740,000 advanced agricultural cooperatives, embracing 99 per cent of the peasantry, had been engulfed by 26,000 (later consolidated into 24,000) communes.

"Management councils were set up by the former township governments and party committees. In effect they

_____
* *The Chinese Communes,* published by Soviet Survey (London).

became 'organs of state power,' or 24,000 'states within the state.' Commune administrations took over direct management of trade and commerce, small industries, bookkeeping, banking, marketing and supply, education, communal dining halls and kitchens, housing, medical care, the training and command of the militia, as well as public works."

There wasn't much left of the family unit, so recently so all-important in China.

This type of communization did not work. The Great Leap Forward failed. Whether that sort of collectivization will ever work is more than doubtful; it is certainly not what democratic socialists want. It was premature in China and was accompanied by errors in planning. The Party leadership—Mao's dictatorship was never as "personal" as Stalin's—rather promptly decided on retreat under new orders. Snow writes:

"Ownership 'by the whole people' was no longer something to be attained in 'three to five years' but had to await completion of industrialization. That would take 'fifteen, twenty or more years.' Until then China as a whole would remain in a stage of 'socialist construction'—although as the communes built and financed public projects those would, of course, be owned by all. Meanwhile people would work indefinitely for wages; those who had begun a 'free supply' system were wrong. Food was to be considered part of wages, payments for work would be divided into six or eight grades, and peasants would be supplied in accordance with skill and output. A system of rewards was to be enforced.

"Other incentives were restored. The communes which had declared personal possessions—such as bedding, furniture, cooking utensils, bicycles—'public property' were ordered to rescind the proclamation; where such property had actually been seized it was to be returned immediately to its

rightful owners. The working day was acknowledged to be
too heavy. A guarantee of 'eight hours of sleep and four
hours for meals and recreation, altogether twelve hours' was
declared a minimum, even in busy planting and harvesting
seasons. The use of community dining rooms and nurseries
and kindergartens became optional. Existing houses were to
be restored to private ownership, and members could live in
them 'always.' Decisions to build new housing could be taken
only by the villages themselves. Such housing should be con-
structed so that 'the young and aged of each family can all
live together.' The integrity of the three-generation family
was thus reaffirmed."

Among other things, official opposition to birth control
was changed. The population problem could not be ignored, nor could any easily attainable improvement in
agriculture provide the margin of food to cope with the
more or less widespread and frequent periods of flood or
drought.

American *amour propre* was wounded by the success of
the communist revolution over Chiang Kai-shek; hatred
of it grew out of Chinese intervention in behalf of the aggressive North Korean communist government. Our government has steadily supported the absurdity that Chiang
should represent in the UN a China from which he was
ignominiously driven but which some day he pretends he
may re-conquer. In fact, he represents only our Seventh
Fleet; his soldiers imposed themselves on Formosa where
he has never dared to permit any "national" plebiscite,
and where his rule was made tolerable only by extensive
American aid. The U.S. government has used what economic pressure it could to weaken the communists and
has refused to grant us possibly gullible citizens pass-
ports so that we are prevented from observing at first hand

what is happening in the most populous nation on the earth. We are told almost simultaneously by spokesmen for the official line that Communist China is the outstanding danger to the future—which may be true—and that its economic weakness grows ever more apparent.

In grim fact China was strong enough easily to bring remote and hitherto autonomous Tibet under its revolutionary power. That human divinity, the Dalai Lama, and thousands of his devoted countrymen today are refugees in India.

Against India, the Chinese army showed great strength and skill in the border fighting in the high mountains. The army, in the opinion of many observers, could have rather easily cut through to the Bay of Bengal. But Peiping stopped the advance, renounced the desire for conquest, boasted of peaceful treaties on boundaries with Pakistan and all its other neighbors except India, and proposed negotiations on disputed territory. Peiping refused, however, to withdraw as far as the Indians wished because the positions its troops occupied gave them strategic advantages. Thus the Sino-Indian quarrel is added to the world's warbreeding crises and India's moral and political influence as a "neutral" has greatly lessened.

Meanwhile, and even more significantly, there has been a steadily growing rift between the great Communist Powers—the U.S.S.R. and China. It is an ideological rift. The Chinese have taken the role of unreconstructed Stalinists —or Leninists—who believe that *the* enemy is still capitalist imperialism, not the danger of nuclear war. The U.S. is the incarnation of the prevailing imperialism. Khrushchev was soft in yielding to the U.S. and removing missiles from Cuba.

Khrushchev, with the support of all the communist parties in Europe, except little Albania, has abandoned the dogma of an inevitable explosion of capitalism in war. He does not believe that socialism will automatically emerge out of the ruins of thermonuclear war; he does believe in the possibility of communist victory without nuclear war; his communism has now become generally "softer" than the newer Chinese brand.

Along with this genuine ideological difference undoubtedly goes a power conflict for leadership in the communist bloc. The religion of nationalism is by no means dead in the communist world. China has reason to look to Outer Mongolia and Central Asia as regions for Chinese influence, regions which might absorb her excess population and perhaps ultimately become annexes.

Unquestionably this break in monolithic communism introduces a new element into the cold war between the West and the East, more especially between the U.S.A. and the U.S.S.R. The great Powers cannot look with favor on dispersal of nuclear weapons. China, it is believed, is on the verge of her first nuclear test. It is thought that she may become a nuclear power by 1970. With her advance in technology, she probably will be a more effective rival of the U.S., the West, *and* the U.S.S.R. for influence in the underdeveloped nations caught in the revolution of rising expectations. Should this situation occur, the very life of mankind may depend upon bringing her to agree to disarmament. Is that possible?

No one can give a positive, affirmative answer. But one can say that it is impossible in view of America's policy of excluding China from the U.N. Nor is our talk of disarmament encouraging while our government is steadily in-

creasing its own budget for arms and piling up weapons
of overkill. It is not, as some speculate, by a future military alliance of Russia and the West against China—a
doubtful eventuality—that the world will be spared, but
by a combined effort to persuade her to join in general
disarmament. (De Gaulle must be brought in.) If the Chinese government means what it says, it is opposed to nuclear arms and nuclear war. In the *People's Daily* of December 31, 1962, one of China's first open statements of
opposition to Khrushchev and one of the most vigorous
condemnations of the U.S., occurs this statement:

> "It would be an unprecedented calamity for mankind if
> nuclear war should break out. It is precisely for this reason
> that we have always called for a complete ban on nuclear
> weapons; that is, a total ban on the testing, manufacturing,
> stockpiling and use of nuclear weapons."

Moreover revolution in China is subject to the same
softening influences as have affected revolution in Russia;
the very success of communism in raising living standards
at home may make government, and certainly the people,
as reluctant as the nations of the West seriously to consider
resorting to thermonuclear war—a war that can hardly be
avoided except by general disarmament. Socialist internationalism must stress this hope of disarmament and a
peaceful approach to the Chinese danger.

As a movement with a missionary ideology—I had almost written, "as a church"—communism has made impressive progress, above ground and underground, in nations which are trying to climb out of the abyss of poverty.
Communist emissaries are devoted, persuasive and unscrupulous. Their formula is to fan the unrest of poverty's vic-

tims who can then be exploited or guided toward communism.

The whole subject of socialism for nations burdened by poverty, and, in many cases, by overpopulation, requires later consideration. Here it must be observed that many of these nations are disposed to playing the East vs. the West, and thus to receive aid without committing themselves to either side. Revolt has been harder to develop into positive communism than Khrushchev may have thought.

Walter Z. Laqueur, the perceptive and well informed editor of the British magazine, *Survey* (a Journal of Soviet and East European Studies), says (in the issue of June, 1962) concerning the schism in communism and the growth of what he calls "polycentrism," "the fact that the very success of communism in the under-developed countries seems to be its undoing. It has been adulterated and produces a strange harvest; under a veneer of Marxist-Leninist ideology, of anti-imperialist slogans, state control of the economy and one-party rule, influences are at work which have very little to do with Marxism or even Leninism. Communism is Africanized and Asianized even faster and more thoroughly than Christianity, because it is a secular movement and therefore in greater need of adaptation. The outcome is a mixture of communist elements and components alien to it. This, from the point of view of communist unity, is highly regrettable, but the irony of it is that any progress by world communism can now be achieved only by strengthening the centrifugal trends and thus weakening the movement from within."

In this connection it is significant that the Indian Communist Party backs its fatherland, not China.

The effect of this polycentrism on communism, both in

theory and in action, may be very great. For one thing, if international unity cannot be obtained under one pope in Moscow, what will become logically of the argument that within each country communists must permit only one unified party?

If Laqueur's piece had been written after the Cuban crisis of October 1962, when we stood on the very brink of thermonuclear war, he might have added that communism is Cubanized, or, shall we say, Latin-Americanized, as well as Africanized and Asianized. When Kennedy and Khrushchev went over Castro's head and ended the acute crisis, Castro did not say, "Khrushchev has given, Khrushchev has taken away, blessed be the name of Khrushchev." Experts on Cuba are still debating whether Castro concealed the fact that his successful revolution was communist inspired and waited for an appropriate time to admit it, or whether his adoption of communism was at least partially the result of American policy and its effect on his temperament. At any rate, he more or less escaped the pains of American discipline by turning to Moscow. Khrushchev's handling of the crisis of bases and missiles was certainly a blow to Castro's pride. He did not—indeed he could not—break with Moscow, but his dependence on the Kremlin by no means made him a completely docile satellite. In *The Reporter* (January 17, 1963) that authoritative student of Cuban affairs, Theodore Draper, writes, "He (Castro) has apparently staked out for himself a Communist sphere of influence all his own in Latin America and offered to take a mediatory position between Soviet Russia and Communist China on a world scale."

It is Cuba, as a center of subversion in Latin America, that most disturbs Washington now. The danger is not imaginary. But the continuing great propaganda for communism among our neighbors is less due to Castro's efforts than to the refusal of unstable governments to make reforms without which Mr. Kennedy's Alliance for Progress will not work. It will be difficult to atone for the blunders and errors of Yankee capitalist imperialism in this hemisphere. The answer to communist progress will not come from fighting it with bombs. The answer to communism in the world can be derived from a more effective socialism. Will we offer it?

VII.

Marxism's Inadequacies

THIS BOOK raises a number of questions pertaining to democratic socialism and communism, the answers to which—many communists and some socialists believe—can be derived from a more concentrated study of Marxism. I am tremendously impressed by Marx's role in history and by the power of Marxism as a "mystique" in much of today's world.

As I have already indicated, I do not believe that every word of Marx and Engels should be regarded as fundamentalist Christians regard the Bible. Marx's thinking has greatly affected the world we live in. But this is not his world, despite the wide popularity of Marxism. The age of nuclear energy and cybernetics is much different from the age of improved and glorified steam engines. Today's population explosion cannot be dismissed as Marx dismissed Malthus. In general, Marxists in power or on the road to power have had to read into, rather than derive from, Marx their programs of practical action. Our thinking about ourselves has been greatly affected by Freud, Adler, and their disciples and, more than we realize, by our experiences in two world wars. It isn't easy to fit the results tidily into the Marxist framework.

Nevertheless men, even revolutionaries, love to have authority to which they can appeal, and Marx still is an authority in the opinion of millions, most of whom have little firsthand knowledge of his theories. Let us take a brief look, then, at how some of his more important dogmas stand in the light of recent events.

1. His doctrine of materialist determinism of history. That is a philosophical notion which is not essential to modern socialism. One may accept the important truth that we and our institutions are greatly conditioned by the way in which our society makes its living, yet hold to a divergent underlying philosophy. Marx's view may have given philosophical support to the dream that a socialist economy would automatically enable men to live like brothers, without crime. Today, Marxism may, in a sense, fill a theological void for communist atheists, but in democratic socialist thinking it has by no means abolished ethics or made them negligible, nor has it dehumanized man.

In our day, the unconscionable struggle for power has been the outstanding foe of decent social morality, and has gone along with a wide range of beliefs about man and his relation to the universe. Of itself, Marx's materialist determinism no more abolished ethics than a stern Calvinist predestination abolished them. Marx scorned ethical and religious socialists. His followers were to be scientific. But I can testify to the high quality of socialist ethics of dedicated men and women, many of them Marxists, who, by no means regarded themselves or their fellow human beings as puppets of their materialist heredity and environment. Marx himself believed that man was the subject rather than the object of history, and, at least in his

younger years, was profoundly concerned by the alienation of the individual from his hopes and from society.
This goal of a society in which everyone contributed according to ability and received according to need has an
ethical quality of the highest sort.

2. Marx held that history is a progression of social orders, each born from the womb of the preceding. Unquestionably socialism owed much of its strength and appeal
to the feeling of assurance that its doctrine gave to the
exploited. It was a view of history that did for the poor
what the faith that they were God's chosen did for Moslems and Calvinists. We are so made that we fight better
and harder for that which we are sure is fated to win. In-
tellectually the doctrine is plausible and roughly corresponds to European history. But only roughly. It has
served better as an explanation of the past than as a definite guide to present conduct, as socialists discovered when
faced with the triumph of Marxism in quasi-feudal Russia
and in China, rather than in the highly industrialized, capitalist nations of Western Europe. Moreover, Marx seemed
to think, rather arbitrarily, that this principle of continuing
change would be ended forever in the communist utopia
which he suggested rather than described. Why? He did
not explain.

3. Marx's theory of immiseration (horrible word). Theoretically, this theory meant that more and more persons
under capitalism would be pressed down into the status
of wage workers and consequently into greater and greater
misery. This was a part of the process destined to lead to
revolution. I have read and heard some modern Marxists
casuistically try to explain this theory in terms consistent
with present facts. In so doing, I think they are twisting

Marx's meaning and making a poor case. Capitalism is
still failing to provide and to share the plenty which modern science and technology make possible. Even in the
richest of countries, our own, the differences are economically as well as morally indefensible. Nevertheless, in the
Western world, the material lot of the workers is vastly
better than it was one hundred years ago. Machinery more
and more supplants brute manpower, and even brain
power; the percentage of labor in the sense of wage workers in factories is diminishing.

4. The class struggle. In popular Marxism, this held the
highest place. It was something the workers could feel.
Differences between rich and poor, owners of land and machinery and those who had nothing save hunger and ability, had long been felt in the Western world. The wonder
was that the hatred these differences aroused did not more
frequently result in aggressive action. Yet the class struggle never could bear the weight popular Marxism put
upon it. Certainly it cannot today. That is to say, a nearly
automatic class struggle between two major classes, probably will not be consciously realized and certainly will not
of itself bring a desirable socialism. A vulgar Marxist class-
conflict doctrine was baldly expressed by none other than
the anti-socialist, Samuel Gompers, long the able leader
of the A.F.L., who collaborated extensively with capitalists. Asked by Morris Hillquit, his socialist opponent in a
debate, to describe his program for the workers, he replied
that it was simply "more and more and more" for them.
Logically, that meant an endless struggle against ownership, a struggle which lacked any constructive plan or
program. (He spoke mostly for a kind of labor elite
organized in craft unions and far from united with the

workers of lower economic levels.)

It is clear that the class struggle, even if it is successful, is only one of many social struggles. Although it may
greatly influence other social struggles, it by no means
wholly explains or controls them. Plain hunger, and other
pressing material wants, have set tribe against tribe and
nation against nation in violent conflict, far more often
than class against class.

As H. J. Muller points out, Egypt, in 3,000 years of
history, fought numerous wars, apparently without violent
class struggle. Religions and religious conflicts have
greatly affected our history, and cannot be ascribed
wholly to masked class conflicts. Granting the interaction
of religious with economic systems, notably of Roman
Catholicism with feudalism, and of Protestantism with
capitalism, it stretches interpretation to the breaking point
to see in religious struggles nothing but masked class
conflict.

It is even more difficult thus to explain the rise of the
comparatively modern religions of absolute sovereign national states, for which in our time so many millions have
killed or have been killed. "Workers of the world unite;
you have nothing to lose but your chains; you have a
world to gain," had an enormous emotional appeal, but
it has been and still is about as ineffective in international
politics as the proclamation of Christian brotherhood. If
the world's workers have chains in common, they vary
in weight. World Wars I and II—and III, if it comes—
cannot be explained simply in terms of *the* class conflict.
There are other conflicts.

In the United States, where raw class conflict in great
strikes is much more obvious than in some far more so-

cialist nations, well organized unions are now very much a part of the established order. Collectively, these unions own a great deal of capital. They have many guaranteed financial benefits and the great right of collective bargaining. Their standards are middle-class standards, which fact is proved by the high salaries received by union officers. Before the coming of the New Deal, I regarded labor as a kind of surrogate for humanity in its struggle to organize and better itself. I could almost say that every strike was morally justified even if not always tactically wise. I cannot say that today, even though I am a member of organized labor (American Newspaper Guild), and am hopeful that labor unionism will be extended to the millions of now unorganized workers.

The class struggle in the U.S.A. is complex, and involves a variety of labor groups; thus sometimes internecine strife develops between rival unions in the same overall A.F.L.-C.I.O. This labor complex is part of that cold war military-industrial complex against which President Eisenhower warned us.

The best one can say about the great A.F.L.-C.I.O. is that it is sufficiently haunted by the plight of the unorganized workers, yes, and humanity, to adopt some good resolutions, and to spend some money here and abroad in aid of the world's workers. Its official stand against race discrimination is good, but it is by no means practiced by many of its constituents at the local level. Race solidarity, however pitiful, is still more important in the Deep South than unity of workers. This is also true in other parts of the country. But the situation is improving. Almost 50 years ago, an A.F.L. organizer, who later rose in its service, after perfunctorily addressing despairing strikers, most of whom were immigrants of many national origins, said to me, "Well, that's over. My wife says when I come home she can tell by the smell on my clothes what kind of Hunkies or Wops I've been talking to." I do not think a labor man of any standing could say that today.

There is another very important consideration which tends to lessen the practical appeal of over-simplified class conflict: owners vs. workers. That is the evidence on both sides of what Churchill first called the Iron Curtain that social or government ownership by no means solves all problems for the workers. There is the question of management. In the state as well as in industry and collectivized agriculture, management constitutes what Djilas has called the "Third Class." Backed by the state, this "third class" is more powerful in communist countries than any class in those democratic nations which have not abolished capitalism. Once fairly decent wages and working conditions are established, it matters comparatively little to the average worker—a coal miner, for instance—whether the owner is the state or a corporation. Both are to them, absentees. The worker's *they*, as opposed to his *we*, is management with which the worker comes face to face. Socialists have not given this problem adequate consideration. We shall return to it. For now, suffice it to mention the way automation may be changing the psychology of the class conflict. In many lines the worker himself will become the manager of the machine which has displaced many human beings, and made more acute the overall problems of employment and leisure.

To sum up this brief discussion, I have long been of the opinion that we must consciously stress the appeal of

socialism to the consumers as advantageous to their interests; that is, advantageous to all of us who want our
natural resources and the skill of men to be utilized for
the conquest of poverty and for the enrichment of our
common life. There were—there still are—socialist syndicalists and labor organizations such as the Industrial
Workers of the World in America, who raised the cry, "All
power to the producers," usually meaning wage workers
and their leaders. My old friend, Dr. James Warbasse, a
skilled surgeon, persuaded the I.W.W. to accept him as a
manual worker. He accepted the cry, "All power to the
producers," but soon shifted it to "All power to the consumers," and worked for the cooperative movement. I
could not follow him so far. But today, a consumers'
socialism, or more accurately, an emphasis on what we all
need: peace, freedom, and modest abundance, will further
democratic socialism in this violent world more than will
beating the drums of class struggle. What we need is a
society in which all of us share equitably in production
and consumption. We have to think both as producers and
consumers.*

4. Marxist theory of value and surplus value. Assuredly,
this remains to be discussed in economic theory. In pure
Marxist form—if Marx gave it a pure form—it is not accepted by most socialist economists, who differ in their
degree of amendment of and zeal for it. It does not seem
to me to be of much help in our great problem of providing machinery for industrial progress. Practically, our

* In the spring of 1962 Jerry Voorhis, executive director of the Cooperative League of the U.S.A. pointed out that in the U.S. there are
nearly five million member-owners of electric cooperatives and more
than twelve million members of the credit unions. Consumers' cooperation
—which long ago won socialist blessing—is in various forms very strong
in a great many nations.

problem is this: labor is entitled to what it creates; that
is, to what cannot be made without labor. But labor needs
expensive machinery. In a live economy, there must be
steady capital investments in the great tools of production. This must come somehow out of the national product. So must support of the national defense and general
welfare. The whole product (as, of course, Marx knew)
cannot be divided into wages to be used for individual
consumption. How shall working capital be obtained?
By inducement of individual or corporate saving and investment, or by government appropriation through ownership or taxes? How much planning, by whom and how?
Labor as labor, and certainly as part of the consuming
public, has heretofore gained, in the long run, through
capital investment, but at great cost, whether as in the
original British model through its exploitation by private
capitalism or as in Russia through its exploitation by the
state. In this age of automation in which thousands of
workers are being displaced and in which the very nature
of work is changing, Marx's theory of value and surplus
value is of little practical help.

5. Marx's doctrine of the state and the dictatorship of
the proletariat. Socialists have been divided and troubled
by this issue. Marx's own theory was not clear enough to
escape sharply conflicting interpretations. Discussions of
"the state," socialist and non-socialist, usually depend
upon the particular aspect of it uppermost in the minds
of the discussants at the time. As eagerly as syndicalist
socialists want the welfare state to surrender its functions
to one big union, our ultra conservatives also want it to
wither away, and would be—they say—content to leave
most of its essential functions to the mythical goddess,

"free enterprise," with corporations and chambers of commerce as her ministers.

But these same conservatives are devout worshipers of the state as the sovereign military god of the religion of nationalism. Few of those who mouth the time-honored sentiment that that government is best which governs least, will hesitate to ask government for any favor which would be beneficial to their own special interests. The social organization declared incompetent to function in the economic field is called upon by many of its critics to control thought, speech and the published word.

Man's inherent nature has made government an essential facet of society. We have always had some sort of government under some sort of elite, and probably always will. The character of the government and of the elite has been profoundly affected by the dominant economy. The state has been an agent of the "dominant" economic class. But the highly developed state of our day cannot be explained simply as the agent of a ruling class which will die with the victory of the working class. If it does, it will be merely a semantic death. The business of living together decently in a complicated world will continue to require, for a long time to come, the institution we now call the state. And with the state, we shall have bureaucracy (that is, workers in its service), and an elite. Our hope is to improve their quality and their responsiveness to an increasingly intelligent democracy. In some respects, the state will continue, as it obviously does today, to increase its activities. Who else can act? It is our business to see that it acts as our great servant, not as our master. That this is possible is proved by the solid gains the masses have made in democratic welfare states.

It has not been true that nothing can be done by and for the workers without dissolving the "capitalist" state.

Sanction of the state will be the result of the necessary services it renders, not as heir of a mystical, divine right of kings. Its national sovereignty will be abridged, we hope, by increased interdependence. Its destructive fury in war will end with the growth of a federation of peoples whose laws will preclude coercion or threat of coercion. As a matter of right, voluntary associations and organizations should coexist with and supplement the state—without the state utilizing its coercive powers.

"Withering away" is a poor description of what we ought to desire of the democratic state. The notion that the freedom we want can be promoted by the dictatorship of the proletariat runs counter to logic, common sense and painfully observed facts in communist countries. Rosa Luxemburg's dream of a working class dictatorship, itself internally governed democratically, to guide the people to a classless and ultimately stateless society, cannot work. Dictatorship of a party, ultimately of a man, does not abolish the state, but makes it a more cruel and absolute master. Freedom for men in society cannot be attained through dictatorship, but in opposition to it.

Democracy is indeed an acquired grace. Its price is intelligent vigilance by the people. Its forms may not always be the forms of Western parliamentary democracy, nor will they peacefully evolve under personal rule, such as Nkrumah is developing in Ghana, under which there is less civil liberty than there was under British colonialism. But, whatever our difficulties, our hope for freedom throughout the world depends upon the acceptance of the ideals of democracy and on a conscious, active effort to achieve them.

My appraisal of Marxism shows why I am not a Marxist. It leaves room for great appreciation of what Marx's teaching has meant for men. I have had enough training in theological casuistry, Christian and socialist, to find my way under the general umbrella of Marxism, but not by that process do I think I can best state what the highest meaning of socialism is to me, and, I hope, to others. The answer to the special problems of our times for socialism does not lie in more extensive Marxist exegesis. This is especially true in the U.S.A.

VIII.

Socialism in the U.S.A.

IT IS RATHER the fashion to regard American socialism as quite different from the socialism of its European
comrades, and it is felt that American socialists are inept
at solving their problems. Actually, European and American socialisms present similar problems: gradualism or
reformism vs. revolution, anarchism or syndicalism, or
use of the state. American socialist platforms from 1900
on were combinations of "immediate demands" for reforms (most of which, after some fashion, were later taken
over by the old parties), and revolutionary proposals for
a new society, similar to those made in Europe. As in
Europe, anarchists and syndicalists challenged any reli-
ance on, or even any use of, the state. The movement
exhibited a genius for factionalism.

The American party, born with the century, had considerable appeal in its early years. It began with a coalition of Midwestern Social Democrats and New York dissenters from the dogmatic syndicalism of Daniel De Leon
and his Socialist Labor Party. Socialism of some form was
then by no means new in America. It had seen many
voluntary collectives wax and wane under religious, cultic,

113

humanitarian, or socialist inspiration. (Such socialist experiments were influenced more by Robert Owen's socialism than Marx's.) Marx himself had been a correspondent of Horace Greeley's *New York Tribune*. The First International had been allowed to die in New York.

There was much native radicalism in America's history and tradition, and by 1900, a great deal of exploitation, which Marxism recognized and sought to remedy. The established parties, Republican and Democrat, had no competitive cures to offer, and even after the advent of progressivism, and Theodore Roosevelt, they were slow to adopt any sweeping reforms. Socialism in its various European forms was very much in the air.

Hence the new party, blessed with a worker's hero like Gene Debs, five times socialism's candidate for President, with leaders and theorists of the stature of Morris Hillquit in New York and Victor Berger in Wisconsin, and with writers like Jack London, Upton Sinclair and others, made real progress.

On the eve of World War I, a total of 667 party officials held public office. These were divided as follows: state legislators, 21; mayors, 34; aldermen, 230; other municipal officers, 106; county officers, 150; school officers, 126.

Socialism's opposition to American entry into the war at first added to its membership.

In 1963, I recall these figures with considerable pain, the more so because I was our Party's principal leader—six times its candidate for President—from 1928 through 1948. I think I speak objectively when I say that I do not think my own mistakes or the factionalism which attended and followed the communist split, were chiefly responsible.

Despite its progress in the Debs years, the Party never had the appeal that socialism had in Western Europe. The official labor movement—the American Federation of Labor—was predominantly indifferent or hostile to it. (Nevertheless, socialists had a greater role in building and inspiring the labor movement than some labor historians will admit.)

There were two reasons for the party's moderate appeal: first, in a country of expanding frontiers, blessed with plenty of land, peopled by successive waves of immigration, mostly free of a landed aristocracy, class feeling was never as strong as it was in Europe. From this sprang the second reason: comparatively fortunate and ambitious men could rise out of their class more easily than they could help their class to wipe out the economic basis for classes.

The socialist movement, therefore, was not so firmly rooted that it could withstand the strains of persecution precipitated by World War I and the communist split. Its partial recovery in the Great Depression could not make it strong enough to withstand the appeal of Roosevelt's New Deal, which appropriated many of its immediate demands. And in the process of doing so, it successfully removed a socialist taint so that even Republicans accepted most of it, while protesting with straight faces their devotion to "free enterprise."

Yet this is not the whole story. The Great Depression, out of which sprang the New Deal, was the failure of a system. (In 1932, Hoover was widely and unfairly credited—or discredited—for being responsible for the Depression. A popular parody of the 23rd Psalm, which was widely circulated, began, "Hoover is my shepherd, I shall do nothing but want." I used to tell audiences that neither Hoover nor any one man was big enough to produce so big a depression. It was the system which had produced it.)

Earlier, the system had produced Populism with its agrarian radicalism. In 1912, Bull Moose Progressivism arose, under the leadership of the former President, Theodore Roosevelt. The radical syndicalist-socialist I.W.W. flowered among many workers before World War I. Anarchy itself made its impression on the public.

The Great Depression produced not only the moderate Franklin D. Roosevelt and the New Deal, but immoderate and demagogic radicals, semi-fascists like Huey Long of Louisiana and Father Coughlin of Detroit.

The year 1948, after the New Deal's establishment, witnessed a strong protest party movement, headed— but not for long—by Henry Wallace, and considerably manipulated by communists. It was doomed to rapid death despite its apparent initial strength by its failure to win wide support at the election which saw Truman's triumph in his "give 'em hell" campaign.

All these and other efforts were mere flashes in the pan, or at least have been reduced, like the I.W.W. today, to shadows of their former strength. The Prohibition Party, which had more to its platforms than its main issue of ending the liquor traffic, had political strength until the Anti-Saloon League tactics appeared to enthusiasts to be more effective. But none of these movements, at the height of its influence and popularity, won enough permanent support to challenge the two established parties. No third party has ever grown like an oak from an acorn. The Republican Party is no exception. It became a second party in its first national election, it was the Whig Party

which died. Why has there been this general failure of
"third" parties?

The reasons are largely political and are to be found in
America's history, and its Constitution. I have sometimes
told English friends that had we had a centralized parliamentary government rather than a federal presidential
government, we should have had, under some name or
another, a moderately strong socialist party.

President Kennedy, reflecting on what a Democratic
Congress has done to his program, might, with some
justice, challenge my calling ours a presidential government. It is near enough to it in that the choice of the
President is the major all-absorbing political issue. He is
the man for or against whom everybody votes, or thinks
he votes. But in legal form, citizens vote not directly for
the presidential candidate, but for a college of electors.
Each state has as many electors as it has representatives,
plus its two senators. The system is so arranged that
voting strength of small states is disproportionately high.
In voting for electors, the citizens do not vote under
uniform qualifications or rules for getting candidates on
the ballot, but under the various laws and procedures of
fifty states, some of which make it virtually impossible for
a minor party to get or stay on the ballot. To be elected,
especially in our times, a candidate must be backed by
a party strong enough to raise millions of dollars. A single,
hour-long, syndicated television program, costs more than
the Socialist Party had in funds during any of my six
campaigns.

To win, the candidate must win a majority vote of the
electoral college, or, failing that, the election goes to the
House of Representatives, in which each state has one

vote, thus enormously increasing the already dispropor-
tionate electoral weight of the less populous states. Three
times the candidate with the popular plurality has lost.
In 1948 a small shift in three close states, Ohio, Illinois
and California, would have elected Dewey, without destroying Truman's substantial plurality. The average
American voter wants to take no chance on this. He may
prefer a minor party candidate, but will cast his vote for
one of the two major party candidates. His decision is
based on how much he likes, or learns to like, one of the
candidates, or on how much he dislikes or hates one
candidate more actively than the other. Almost up to
election day, he may think he will vote for his real
preference, a minor party candidate who managed to get
on the ballot in his state, but then he will decide that he
can't take a chance, "lest that so-and-so get in." (How
often I have been told just that!) If the President of the
United States could be elected by a popular preferential
ballot in which the voters numbered their choices, the
Socialist Party would be a force to be reckoned with at
the polls.

This opinion is bolstered by many considerations, one
of them the fact that Gene Debs got his highest vote—
6 per cent of the total—in 1912. Why? Partly, at least,
because that year, voters were pretty sure that the winner
would be Woodrow Wilson or Theodore Roosevelt, not
William H. Taft, and they didn't believe that the difference between these two fairly progressive men was important enough to prevent their voting for their real
preference, the outspoken socialist and labor man, the
beloved Gene Debs. In 1916, when the Party itself was
stronger, they gave no such vote to Allan Benson, the

socialist candidate. For one thing, he wasn't Debs, but that is not the whole story.

It is easier to make the sort of choice I have described because of the logical absurdities of our two-party system. Each of them is a federation of state parties, held together by historic and sociological considerations, rather than by ideological principle. The leaders of both parties, especially the Democratic, since 1932, have shown considerable willingness to adopt measures once considered socialist or almost socialist. Within each party, differences are greater than, on the average, between them, so that one asks of a candidate for Federal office not so much whether he is a Democrat or a Republican but what kind of a Democrat or Republican. Labor, since 1932, is fairly content that it has kept and increased its gains by picking individuals (usually Democrats), who, by conviction or for the sake of labor votes, will come nearest to its demands. It runs its political campaigns on this principle with fair, but far from total success.

The differences between the parties are sociological rather than philosophical. Let an observer find out the sex, geographical location, occupation, national origin, church connection of an American citizen, and, nine times out of ten, he can determine the voter's party preference. However, it by no means follows that the citizen will always vote according to the label.

Insofar as the parties claim to have historic principles, they have swapped them. On the whole, except in the South, the Democratic Party tends to support very strong federal government, while the Republican Party—with exceptions—mourns the continuing decline of state's rights. Alexander Hamilton, Abraham Lincoln, Thomas

Jefferson, John C. Calhoun, would all be surprised by today's political parties. So little are the voters accustomed to honest thinking in terms of political preference, that the average Democrat and Republican, if asked to give reasons for voting as he does, wouldn't know what you were talking about.

If this extraordinary irrationality of our parties and lack of sharp division between them made it possible, under strong leadership like Roosevelt's in time of crisis, to work out a pragmatic peaceful near-social revolution, it has also made possible the flouting, not only of the advanced Democratic platform of 1960, but of most of the Democratic President's program by a Democratic Congress in which the generally conservative Southern Democratic senators and representatives hold, by virtue of seniority, most of the important committee chairmanships.

In spite of a political set up in which the cards are stacked against a third party, had Roosevelt's New Deal not given us a welfare state, which was in no way indicated by his 1932 campaign platform, the Socialist Party, the Communist Party, and perhaps some new party compounded of enthusiasts for Huey Long and Father Coughlin, would have acquired political strength. Roosevelt's great public support was not won during his first campaign, but began with his inaugural address in 1933. He was elected the first time simply because he wasn't Mr. Hoover, but that was not the only reason for his popularity. The New Deal averted popular disturbances of a serious sort, without solving the problems it ameliorated or without giving us the improvements in the mechanics of democracy which we needed.

Our Constitution is indeed a remarkable document with

a remarkable history. No other contemporary nation has lived so long or so well under the same written constitution. Ours went into effect in 1789, with the inauguration of George Washington. Its vitality is to be explained because under vigorous leadership at critical times, and a broad judicial interpretation, its checks and balances did not slam the brakes on peaceful progress. (The Civil War was the terrible exception. Slavery found protection behind the constitutional barrier of states' rights and the Dred Scott decision.)

There was a case for emphasis on checks and balances in 1789, in a federation of rural states on a continent, protected by two great oceans, which scarcely exists today. A government, faced with our problems, has to act. Basic rights of American citizens cannot indefinitely be left at the mercy of states of very unequal size, strength and financial capacity, whose boundaries have little relation to economic realities. New York City, for example, is the vital center of a metropolitan area which includes not only most of four New York State counties outside its boundaries, but substantial parts of New Jersey and Connecticut. Political scientists and economists are going farther and talking about an urban area extending from north of Boston to south of Washington. The cry of state's rights under these conditions is usually raised by conservatives and reactionaries in defense of special interests which fare better under the divided rule of states. The cry is very seldom raised against Federal appropriations to states for highways or other Federal establishment or the support of wasteful state military organizations, but only against Federal aid to education or health or the terribly exploited migratory agricultural workers.

Even more serious today is the relation of the President to Congress, and of both to the people. Believers in democracy, under representative government, are faced with a dilemma. Local regions and local interests should be represented. Over-centralization of power causes real dangers. Nevertheless the sum of varying local interests does not equal the national interest, nor is a valid and progressive decentralization of power served by a congress which is more concerned with local benefits than with the great issues confronting a President. The first Congress of the Kennedy Administration vividly illustrated our problem. Controlled by the President's own party, it was the men nominally elected on his own platform who blocked the larger part of his welfare program. The House was more difficult than the Senate. The two old men, Senator Hayden and Representative Cannon, chairmen, respectively, of the Senate and House Appropriations Committees, for some weeks held up government payments on appropriation bills which, while needing minor adjustments, were passed by both houses.

The House and its chairman wished to assert their equality, if not primacy, in joint conferences on appropriations by quarreling over the choice of the room in which to meet and the man who should preside. It never seemed to occur to them how much valuable time might be saved for members of Congress and interested witnesses on appropriations by beginning with joint hearings on appropriation bills.

Under the weight of public business, it has come to pass that the average representative's chance of election, or, more accurately, re-election, very often depends more on what he can get by way of appointments, jobs, con-

tracts for his district, or the people in it, than upon his
stand on important issues. The youngest Kennedy immor-
talized the slogan "Who can do more for Massachusetts?"
Who, indeed, the voters agreed. Under given House rules
and pressure of business, the average representative hasn't
too much chance anyway to capture public attention by
his speeches or by other work on issues. Moreover, the
House notoriously has over-represented rural and under-
represented the urban population—a matter that finally
may be ended by the recent intervention of the Federal
courts in complaints against the process of gerrymander-
ing of districts by state legislatures.

In these circumstances, national interests are usually
best represented by the President. He cannot be ousted
by congressional disapproval like the British prime minister under the parliamentary system, but neither has the
President anything like such direct control over legislation
as the British chief executive, so long as his party controls
parliament. The prime minister doesn't have to worry
much about two houses—control of the Commons is
enough.

This is not an argument for the parliamentary system
in America, or for turning Congress into an aggregation
of rubber stamps for presidential bills. Still less is it an
argument for a monster effort to change the Constitution
by drastic amendment. Today that would be politically
impossible. Any extensive revision of the Constitution
today would probably be for the worse, especially for civil
liberty. An amendment that I should like definitely to
push at this time would provide for direct election of the
President with uniform rules for putting the names of
candidates for that office on the ballot and uniform qualifi-

cations for voters intended especially to end racial discrimination by various devices under state laws. The amendment should either provide for preferential voting or for a run-off of the two highest candidates, if neither has a majority. The former method would be preferable. We do not want a situation in which one candidate among many on the ballot could be elected by anything less than a true majority. Such an amendment, under our unfortunate constitutional provisions for amendment, would almost certainly be defeated by the votes of the legislatures of the less populous states, which would lose their disproportionately large vote in the electoral college. However, lively discussion of the matter would help. It would be worthwhile to work toward other constitutional amendments, but for now we must rely primarily on presidential leadership.

Effective presidential leadership requires a far more realistic and meaningful realignment of the two great parties. Although strict party discipline is dangerous, parties should be grouped by underlying philosophies and political programs.

For many years I hoped, sometimes against hope, that the Socialist Party and its campaigns could serve as a catalytic agency to stir up and guide the kind of mass awakening which would give us a new party, basically a consciously farmer-labor party, increasingly socialist, and in the process, bring about an opposing conservative party. As late as 1932, there was nothing in the Republican or Democratic national platforms to indicate that this was impossible.

In 1924, we socialists staked a great deal on our gamble that our coalition with some labor and farm organizations and the Wisconsin Progressives would bring about an American farmer-labor mass party strong enough soon to supplant one of the old parties or bring about their merger. We knew that such a party would not immediately be socialist, but we hoped that the logic of the situation, and our efforts, would soon make it so in fact, if not in name.

The odds were always against us, but they multiplied even before the end of a good campaign because some of the labor organizations originally interested, virtually defected. One of the forces that held down the La Follette vote was the cry: A vote for La Follette is a vote to send the election to the House of Representatives.

Now, while I do not affirm the impossibility of the rise of a new party which, substantially would be backed by labor organizations, I think a major party, controlled by labor to the degree that it is in Britain, would be neither attainable nor desirable for reasons I have repeatedly suggested in discussing labor and its relations to socialism in America. Today I do not think that a new mass party, if it is to emerge at all, will call itself a labor party, nor will it be controlled by the same men who control the unions. While a strong new mass party with a socialist philosophy and program may seem remote, such a party may yet come to birth. If so, it will be concerned largely with the road to peace.

After the establishment of the welfare state under Roosevelt, there emerged the possibility that one of the old parties, probably the Democratic, could be helped to evolve into a party at least as socialist as the British Labor Party or the German Social Democrats. This would require either an honorable democratic political solution of

the race problems in the South or a clean-cut break in the
Democratic Party. It would also require the development
of a decided change in the present climate of political
action in the United States. This would begin with an
active minority which accepts the revolutionary belief
that plenty, peace and freedom for all are attainable by
us imperfectly rational men and that to work for them is
to find life's deepest meaning. To that minority, a dedicated socialism should furnish driving power and guidance.

Older generations of American socialists would never
have used such words to frame their role. In Debs' time
they expected the party as such to grow to major strength.
After World War I, under Morris Hillquit's intellectual
leadership, we hoped socialism would become a prime
force in creating a labor or farmer-labor party. Hence, in
1924, the coalition with the La Follette forces, which included the Conference for Progressive Labor Action. With
most of us, the hope for such a party, although postponed,
still lingered.

Meanwhile, to educate the public, or even to keep
socialist ideas alive after the failure of our plans in 1924,
we nominated candidates. The 1932 campaign brought us
new hope and strength, but after 1933, Roosevelt and the
New Deal, communist pressure, and later, fear of nazism
abroad and of fascist tendencies at home, greatly changed
the external situation and socialist and labor reaction to
it. Before 1936, the Party, bedevilled by our internal factions, had lost numerous sympathizers and members of
right and left to the Democrats, or rather, to Roosevelt.
In 1936, a section of the Party split off, nominally on the
question of the way to handle the Communist issue.

Thereupon, in New York (and only in New York) ardent anti-communists, communists, and others, joined in building the American Labor Party, which could strengthen support of Roosevelt. Some years later that party split over the communist issue, and today the secessionists carry on as the Liberal Party, supported by some unions. The American Labor Party died. The Liberal Party exists only in New York State and usually simply nominates Democratic candidates. For this service it gets occasional recognition in nominations and jobs.

The Socialist Party, which remembered how well its opposition to the first world war was justified by events, also opposed entry into the second world war (but not on isolationist grounds). After Pearl Harbor, it gave critical support to the war, and concerned itself with an approach to peace. It was opposed to Roosevelt's simple slogan of unconditional surrender, and to Anglo-American concessions to Stalin in Central Europe.

I am perhaps prouder of our 1944 campaign and its platform than of any of my six presidential campaigns. Unhappily, it did not build the Socialist Party. I ran again in 1948, against my original intention, because I thought that we socialists should not allow the strange conglomeration of the Wallace Progressives, with a minority of communists rather cleverly playing the dominant role, to represent socialism to the American voters.

All this, while state laws, or the way they were enforced, made it harder and harder to stay on the ballot. The popular vote in 1948 was smaller than the reception accorded to me and to my colleague, Tucker Smith, had led us to expect. Wherefore, around 1950, I began a campaign within the Party to utilize our limited resources

of money and manpower in campaigning for socialist
ideas rather than for a presidential ticket doomed to little
notice and humiliating defeat. By 1960, this became the
prevailing opinion of the Party. The majority put its hope
on the political front by working for a meaningful political realignment. Socialists are now allowed by their Party
not only to vote, but to work for those candidates of other
parties who come nearest to the socialist position. The
reasoning behind this is that the welfare state has incorporated a great many socialist "immediate demands."
In doing so, it has precluded, we hope, the necessity of
immediate, if peaceful, internal "revolution." The difference between more or less good or bad political measures
might now be very important, perhaps decisive, in terms
of war or peace. We dare not hope to have an indefinite
number of years free from war during which we can
work for our version of a socialist society which can be
achieved only by complete victory at the polls.

Neither can we afford to allow ourselves or our fellow
citizens to lose sight of the great socialist goal. Within our
American political-economic complex, our efforts to build
a significant numerical force at the polls have failed as
have also our efforts to precipitate a coming of a new mass
party, strongly supported by organized labor. Our devoted efforts in 1952 and 1956 were scarcely noticed except sometimes to be pitied. It was time to look for other
means, to be more flexible in cooperation, to recognize
that the political realignment we wanted could be brought
about by more than one method. At present we can contribute more by persuasively presenting well-thought-out
programs and by campaigning for candidates of a nu-
merically significant party who might be going our way.

We have no intention of following the communist tactics of "boring from within" and denying our true loyalty. The very lack of a principled theoretical basis for either great party makes it possible for an avowed socialist to support those candidates who most accurately represent our ideals, but we must always combine our support with an insistence on the need of better political alignment.

Just how to work out this campaign for realignment is still a subject of much debate within the Socialist Party. I greatly doubt the wisdom of our nominating a presidential candidate. I would like us, however, to be in a position, in congressional campaigns, where old party candidates are very unsatisfactory and we cannot successfully nominate our own, to favor those independent candidates who emphasize our stand on foreign relations. At present, the average Democratic congressman, even one originally well disposed, somehow fails to do this with any vigor because he falls under heavy Administration pressure. Events can change this judgment.

Meanwhile, it is only fair to sympathize with socialists who find it difficult to support any candidate of a "capitalist" or "bourgeois" party. On the practical side they point out the difficulty of maintaining a political party which does not nominate candidates or give voters a chance for a protest vote. They say that it violates our American traditions to call ourselves a party while failing to nominate a presidential candidate. I confess to frequent attacks of nostalgia for those not-so-good old days. It is necessary, however, to change the pattern; to show how a socialist party, under present conditions, can introduce principle and program into political discussion without depleting its limited strength, and without alienating sympathizers by running candidates who would, inevitably, merely draw away votes from the better of the two major party candidates.

I confess that I find myself mourning the days of 1932 when we had the strength and the reason to run a significant campaign, not only for the presidency, but for other offices. I comfort myself with the thought that we contributed much to the improved politico-economic situation in America, unsatisfactory as it is. Further improvement requires different tactics. I do not think one must serve one's Marxist soul by refusing to vote except for one's own Marxist comrades or that by doing so one advances a viable socialism in the nation.

I admire the devotion of members of the syndicalist Socialist Labor Party and the Trotskyist Socialist Workers Party, but I do not approve of their tactical judgments—nor, for that matter, their brands of socialism. My great concern is that we democratic socialists may preserve and enlarge a party whose fellowship will strengthen our own socialism and thus make us effective as isolated individuals cannot be, in serving mankind. Events must guide our program and tactics. Our European comrades believe as much. Witness their participation in coalition cabinet governments. The establishment of a kind of welfare state has changed the situation for socialism, its problems and the tactics it must use to solve them. And this statement leads to a discussion of the kind of program modern democratic socialism should adopt with especial, but not exclusive, reference to the American scene.

IX.

Socialism in Mid-Century

IN RESTATING its philosophy and formulating its program, democratic socialism in the Western nations, and most certainly in the United States, must recognize and explore certain challenges and difficulties:

1. The constant cry that democratic socialism denies liberty. This we can dispose of rather promptly. The liberty that it denies is the liberty of exploitation and the personal enjoyment of special privilege at others' expense. If, by liberty, one refers to Milton's right "to know, to utter and to argue freely, according to conscience," or to our constitutional right of freedom of speech, press, religion and association irrespective of race, creed or color, or to the abolition of such discriminations against Negroes as have disgraced us Americans and our pretensions to equality of right in our culture, then democratic socialists have a good record. We have stood for such freedom in behalf of communists who would deny it to us. We have repeatedly argued the case against such legislation as the

Smith and McCarran Acts.

I remember with joy the cooperation of socialists in
the struggle for civil liberty in our country, but I can't
recall that we fighters for civil liberty ever received much
help from the self-proclaimed champions of freedom
to whom socialism is the bogy. Our economic conservatives, far short of John Birch Society extremism, have not
done conspicuously well for civil liberty. Governments of
the Scandinavian and the British nations, which have been
under socialist party rule, have by no means emulated
communists or fascists in restricting democratic freedoms.

There is, it must be admitted, a deeper problem of the
individual and his freedom of choice and action in a
modern interdependent society. Such a society has its own
pressures for uniformity. They should be less, I think, in
a democratic socialist society than in a society whose
economy is dominated so largely by great corporations
concerned with profit, power, and the cultivation of safe
conformity. But it is true that, as we men are made, liberty
and equality often seem incompatible. One of the constant
tasks of socialism is to wrestle successfully with this
aspect of the problem of the one and the many. It has
been constantly in the back of my mind as I have thought
about socialist programs. One should remember that it is
the equality of legal right and opportunity which should
be cherished. It is not an impossible equality of ability or
of position earned by ability. Socialist economy by no
means should exclude all competition or emulation.

2. The general progress of the welfare state has gradually blurred the once sharp distinctions between the
socialist immediate demands and the programs of increased welfare which non-socialist parties, under various

pressures, are willing to grant through democratic and constitutional procedures. In our complex society, sudden and drastic revolution against a still deep-seated social injustice within our institutions would almost certainly be attended by violence and most certainly by terribly costly confusion. Why, then, socialism, at least in these welfare states?

3. Certain of the most serious problems of democratic socialism, or of democracy itself, do not lend themselves to easy solution by socialist formulas thus far proposed, and sometimes tested in action. Thus, it is clear that ownership of basic industries by the state as agent for society would leave us with questions of relations between management and men; an undemocratic bureaucracy of control in many unions; the exceedingly rapid displacement of workers by automation, much of it in the once better organized occupations; the domination of our economy and our politics by a military-industrial complex, virtually inevitable while the cold war lasts, and while the overriding concern is for national military security.

4. While labor unions are vitally important to the economy and politics of Western nations, their very success has reduced their dynamic propensities for comprehensive socialist change. In general, notably in the United States, organized labor in itself cannot completely represent mankind in a struggle for the kind of justice socialists envision.

5. Finally, and most important of all, is the fact that socialism, as we have known it, does not automatically solve the greatest challenge of our time: the winning of peace. The economics of capitalism is not the sole cause of war, and to supplant it by socialism, nation by nation,

would not necessarily guarantee peace. To quote Paul Henri Spaak, the thing socialists have learned to nationalize best is socialism.

This chapter will be devoted principally to socialism and the welfare state. Has the welfare state made socialism reformist? Should socialism, then, be revolutionary? If so, how? The welfare state has indeed appropriated many measures originally considered socialist. It has acknowledged a national responsibility for unemployment, decent housing, and general health, education and welfare.

But it has been using welfare legislation to cover the inadequacies of a reformed capitalism which failed to conquer poverty because it failed to end essential injustices incorporated in the system. Even as welfare it is inadequate; those who need help most get it least.

It is worth noting that we try to moralize about our system by describing it as a system of free enterprise. Compared to totalitarian system, it is. I repeat one successful economist's observation that the only practitioners of free enterprise in the classic sense are small boys playing marbles for keeps. What free enterprise mostly means to our enterprisers is the right to make a profit. A college student spoke for a great many Americans. When asked what he meant by the noble word, freedom, he said, "My right to try to make as much money as Paul Getty" (the manipulator of oil stocks).

In 1962, the Kennedy Administration, and a Democratic Congress—even more than the Administration—gave interesting proof of this adoration of profit. Our rulers put themselves to much trouble to create a corporation that would help the American Telephone and Telegraph

Company, and others, realize an undeserved profit out of world-wide communication-satellites; all the preliminary scientific and technical work was done by scientists in government employ. A.T.&T. could have been paid to build the Telstar as other organizations were paid for building more complicated satellites. In addition, the government must maintain elaborate controls over this newly created corporation because its work so inevitably involves relations with other nations. All logic of economy and politics called for this international communication to be placed under a public, non-profit-making corporation —somewhat like the very successful T.V.A. But no, in this case, "free enterprise" meant the creation at public expense of a private monopolist corporation that limits the right to make profit to a few only of America's millions. So firmly entrenched is this worship of profit that only nine members of the House voted against it, and public response to an attack on it in the Senate was torpid.

Or take the case of "medicare." The bill pushed by the Administration failed to get the support of Congress. It wasn't a very good bill. It applied only to hospital care for the aged. But it failed, not because of its inadequacies, but because powerful lobbies of private insurance companies and the American Medical Association feared that it would grow into a genuine system of socialized medicine of the sort that has worked so well and proved so popular in Great Britain, the Scandinavian countries and elsewhere. In this day and age, public access to medical help should be much the same as public access to education—not on the basis of a fee-to-doctors system. Britain proves that it need violate no valuable freedom to doctors or patients except the freedom of doctors and private in-

surance companies to grow rich. (British doctors are, as
they should be, very well paid in the context of British
incomes.)

The usual cry of A.M.A. lobbyists was that even government hospital aid to the aged portended the end of
personal freedom and the beginning of the horrors of
George Orwell's *1984*. (You should have heard the young
physician with whom I debated this issue before a high
school class!) John Herling, in his *Labor Letter*, after
deploring the image of the doctor which the A.M.A. is
creating, writes:

> "In fact, the AMA seeks to equate the functioning of the
> medical profession with that of the commercial market
> place. The journal, *Medical Economics*, quotes with ap-
> proval the position taken by Senator Bennett of Utah in
> defending the AMA: 'The American system of private enter-
> prise has resulted in the highest of standards of medical care
> known anywhere. Competition and incentive are factors in
> producing quality, whether in business or in medicine. The
> voluntary American system, although far from perfect,
> shouldn't be sacked because the United States stands alone
> as a bulwark of successful capitalism. In no field—railroads,
> farming, communications, electrical power—has Federal
> control demonstrated superiority over competitive private
> enterprise in the U.S.'
>
> "This, as Nelson H. Cruikshank, director of the AFL-CIO's
> Department of Social Security points out, is the 'bland, un-
> conscious surrender of the standards of a great profession to
> the code of the market place.' Of course, historically, also,
> Bennett's analysis runs wide of the truth."

This sanctification of profit in our welfare state inter-
feres with proper social planning necessary to any economic system in our modern, highly specialized, but in-

terdependent society. The common good cannot be a social byproduct of the desperate struggle for private profit under free competition, out of which, inevitably, have grown overreaching monopolies and oligarchies. Socialist economists have shown how under the general socialist idea of production for common use there is room for something like our present price system for exchange of goods and for private enterprises operated for private profit subject to control by taxation and enlightened labor legislation. American socialists nowadays generally accept, as they should, a mixed economy, controlled by the overall concept that production should be for the good of all. For the state, under any system, to try to own and operate everything, would deprive us of some of the important values of private initiative and responsibility. It would put too heavy a strain on the state. Cooperatives, both of producers and consumers, as alternative forms of social ownership, have their very valuable place.

What, then, about public ownership? I have always said that what the government ought to own depends upon who owns the government. Moreover, priority in extending public ownership depends in part upon special conditions, including the state of public opinion and particular plans for extension. I believe in acquisition by purchase. Obviously, it would be unfair arbitrarily to expropriate some owners without compensation, leaving others to exist as before. Moreover, expropriation invites violence and strife far more costly than compensation. Socialists, however, oppose the business of unloading on the government bankrupt or nearly bankrupt public utilities, and the like at a very high price. (New York City paid an astronomical price for the wobbly corporations which operated its subways.) It is grimly amusing that the state, the target for the arrows of conservative critics, is accepted by many of them as the essential savior of ill-run or ill-fated enterprises, such as the British coal mines and railroads.

What, then, should be owned socially?

The Federal government is, by far, in the best position to organize a socially owned coal, iron, copper, or oil industry. It should be the principal agent of society. But state governments must participate in working out plans because they own much of the land where minerals exist, and because they depend on land taxes to provide funds for education and other functions of local government.

Large forests and acreages of reforested land should be socially owned and socially used, not only for lumber and wood products, but for protection against floods. Woodlots of any considerable size on private farms should be subject to regulation as to use and replanting. Some public ownership of land is necessary for urban planning and slum removal.

The coal mining industry vividly illustrates the practical value of socialization, apart from the ethical objection to private ownership of a natural resource. Some time ago, *Fortune* magazine developed a marvelous, detailed formula for coal mining. Under its formula, coal would be turned into power and heat near the mine mouth; by special process all its by-products would be utilized, thus greatly minimizing waste; mining methods would be safer, and cities and towns would be rid of the smoke nuisance. It would be fantastic to expect so good a plan to be carried out by competing managers of mines of various sizes, whose primary concern is to produce profits for private owners.

Coal and all mineral wealth should be public property, and equally available to all the people. Men may be rewarded for discovering or extracting oil, iron, lead, etc., but they should not own what they did not make. This ownership, ideally, especially in the case of petroleum, should not be so exclusively national as to prevent other nations from benefiting from these resources, except on terms fixed by either national or private owners. Here lies a task for the makers of lasting peace.

As for the surface of the earth, man's desire for a piece of land he can call his own is deeply rooted and widespread. Private ownership of land, with exceptions I have mentioned, should therefore be permitted, but on the basis of occupancy and use. It is axiomatic that the rental value of land is a social creation. I may let my lot go to ragweed, but I can get far more for it than my friend who has cultivated his garden if my lot is located near a town or city. I think socialists might well adopt Henry George's principle that the rental value of land, apart from improvement, belongs to society and should be taxed accordingly. The tax, however, should not be a single tax. This land tax should be supplemented by income and heavy inheritance taxes as the major basis for the support of government and government activities at all levels. Incentive will not be threatened so much by proper tax on land values, as it may be eventually by heavy income taxation. Very heavy inheritance taxes, properly adjusted to care of widows and minor children, would be an expression of justice that would not paralyze incentives.

Wherever efficient production of farm lands requires a plantation or a factory system, there is a strong case for collective ownership and cooperative management.

A remarkable article on the way we have been exploited under our present system and the current real estate boom appeared in *Harper's* magazine, June, 1961. Daniel M. Friedenburg, a successful real estate operator, tells how tax loopholes and our basic doctrine of private ownership are blighting our cities. He quotes with approval a statement in *House and Home* that land speculations have created more millionaires since World War II than any other form of business investment. He tells the story of land bought by his father as a speculation by the *acre* in the 1930's, and sold by him ten years later by the *yard*. "Around 1949, the late Sam Minkoff, a well known builder, bought the same property by the *yard* and after five years was able to sell it by the *foot* making far more money in half the time. And this transaction occurred before the last decade, when over two million people fled the city for the suburbs—making millionaires out of dozens of Long Island potato growers in the process."

The proper management of money or, more accurately, of money, banking and credit ranks in importance with the proper use of land and its mineral wealth. To a great extent, this is already a government function. When Franklin D. Roosevelt first took office, he took over, temporarily, the whole private banking system, which had collapsed. There may be room for some privately owned banks, and more certainly for credit unions or cooperative banks, but the whole Federal Reserve system, or more specifically, all banks of issue, should be owned completely by government, as the agent of society. In a real sense, major decisions on fiscal policy must be political. But the Federal Reserve Board, under socialism, should not be captive to any cabinet minister. It should be free from narrowly partisan political control. I still believe, as I wrote at more length in *A Socialist's Faith,* that we can and should end the system under which generation after generation pays interest to private banks for the social function of creating money in the form of credit.

To this list I should add public utilities, certainly those which serve us best as monopolies. The system of ownership should be flexible, allowing both for extension of T.V.A.-type enterprises, and of the existing successful rural electrification plans.

Steel is the kind of industry which I think should be taken over by government. It is basic to our modern industry; it currently is in the hands of an oligopoly which manages to administer prices with little or no regard for competition. In 1962 President Kennedy felt compelled to crack down on U.S. Steel for its attempt to raise prices after a settlement on wages with the union. Most conservatives and businessmen resented his action as government interference. Would it not be better if the whole steel industry were operated for general use under a public authority similar to T.V.A.? In 1962, labor would probably have said no, chiefly because it would fear that public ownership of the steel industry would deprive it of the right to strike, a matter which will be discussed later.

Extension of public ownership is good, but will not cure all our economic ills. Other steps are necessary. Socialism, far more openly and directly than the welfare state, must challenge the way in which the national income is divided among the people. The noblest ideal would be the Marxist theory "from every man according to his ability, to every man according to his need." For that I am afraid we are not yet ready. And I'm not sure we ever will be. I doubt also whether we are ready for equality of monetary pay. We are, or ought to be, ready to overhaul our present system of apportionment of what the nation produces.

We like to think that now we are rewarded fairly generally according to the value of our work. This is to ignore the large sums paid out to inheritors of wealth, who did nothing to earn it, and to stockmarket speculators who are scarcely better than glorified gamblers. It is also to ignore the capricious way in which value is estimated in terms of monetary reward.

To some extent, pay differentials may reflect differentials in the social values of the work done; far more usually they reflect differences in the uniqueness of the ability a man or woman brings into the market place. He who is endowed by a unique ability to provide what the public needs or wants, will usually be better rewarded for his efforts than if he possessed a similar ability in an even more necessary line of work in which, however, such ability is more common.

Justice in this area is not easily applied. More is necessary, as the Soviet Union abundantly proves, than the dethronement of private profit as economic master. Differentials in salary and wage scales were—and still are —proportionately greater than in the U.S. The communist state knows how to take care of its own. Under any system, it is better to use pay differentials to attract men than to conscript them for jobs.

We in the West are making some progress in the advancement of justice. There is now a floor under wages and salaries prescribed by law, and a ceiling on top of them maintained by taxes. Excessive monetary reward for individual excellence among workers is hindered, if not prevented, by uniformity of wage scales for the same job in factories, offices and schools. Spurs to special individual competence or rewards for it are already mostly other than monetary. It is the over-reward of certain abilities which is rationally ridiculous. Creative work in science and invention has furnished few of our millionaires; the latter are usually administrators or manipulators of stocks or heirs to millionaires. We socialists should give far more attention to progressive, non-violent changes in distribution of the total national—yes—and the world income. The contrast between luxury and poverty, even in affluent America, is a soul-destroying thing. More so, in a world where two-thirds of mankind live on a narrow margin between hunger and starvation.

About the best we democratic socialists can do now is to insist on improvements in the right of collective bargaining, progressive minimum wage laws, and proper income tax legislation. General sales taxes are regressive and fall unfairly on those whose entire income, for the most part, is needed for necessities. Sales taxes on luxury goods are another matter. (When I recommend John Kenneth Galbraith's *Folklore of Capitalism*, and *The Affluent Society*, I try to remember to exempt his support of sales taxes from my praise.)

There is a strong tendency in the U.S. to brush aside theoretical arguments on social justice in our economic system by saying, "Well, don't we live in an affluent society wherein the welfare state, at our expense, keeps everybody from starving?" To such astigmatic viewers of the modern scene, let me recommend an excellent, very readable, little book, *The Other America*, by that good socialist, Michael Harrington.

We boast of progress in fairer distribution of income, but Gabriel Kolko, in his careful, statistical study, *Wealth and Power in America*, gives figures which show that the lowest three-tenths of our working population receive proportionately less personal income before taxes than in 1910. Harrington says that the poor, those below any proper standard of subsistence, now number between 40 and 50 million. Millions of young people start life in a condition of "inherited poverty" and lack of proper health and educational opportunity.

Unemployment among youths is running to 18 per cent; it is a factor in juvenile delinquency and justifies the revival of Civilian Conservation Corps camps—an alleviation, but not a cure.

We are faced with the fact that, because of automation and general technological progress, it is precisely those who drop out of school without special skills who face, under present conditions, something like permanent unemployment. That is an evil whatever the rate of relief.

Reviewing the whole situation in the *New Yorker*, Dwight Macdonald concludes:

" 'Nobody starves' in this country any more, but, like every social statistic, this is a tricky business. Nobody starves, but who can measure the starvation, not to be calculated by daily intake of proteins and calories, that reduces life for many of our poor to a long vestibule to death? Nobody starves, but every fourth citizen rubs along on a standard of living that is below what Mr. Harrington defines as 'the minimal levels of health, housing, food, and education that our present stage of scientific knowledge specifies as necessary for life as it is now lived in the United States.' Nobody starves, but a fourth of us are excluded from the common social existence. Not to be able to afford a movie or a glass of beer is

a kind of starvation—if everybody else can." (Dwight Macdonald, *The New Yorker,* Jan. 19, 1963.)

This whole situation in affluent America, with its flaunt-
ing luxury of the rich, requires a more fundamental approach than the capitalist welfare state will give. It requires not only a far more substantial relief program, but
also a cure going beyond relief. Technical progress does
not necessarily mean social progress. Automation in many
lines will aggravate the problem of unemployment, not
merely of untrained youths, and at least temporarily add
to the population of Mr. Harrington's other America. Automation brings great gains in man's mastery over work, and
will doubtless open new lines of employment. But planning inspired by the socialist ideal is especially necessary
in times of rapid dislocation of workers.

There will be, indeed there should be, further progressive shortenings of the working week, but that alone will
not solve the problem. Our times put heavy emphasis on
the necessity of controlling the introduction of automation, of retraining workers, and of increasing consumption. Such planning will not be infallible. It cannot be
entrusted wholly to government or corporation experts
drawn from bureaucracy and management. Labor must
be drawn into the picture. Socialism's role should be to
insist that such planning be on the principle of a general
increase of goods and services for all, to be equitably
shared by all. This principle can guide us to a use of the
wonders of automation for the common good; the domi-
nance of the profit motive cannot.

But socialism has much work to do in facing the problem. There is no conceivable apocalyptic revolution that

will suddenly do the job. Great violence would be an ugly
and clumsy tool. Here I doubtless shall be told by some of
my friends that I am only talking reformism while socialism is, or should be, revolutionary and that revolution
requires some acceptance of violence.

To which I reply that many of the problems I have discussed will not automatically disappear, however total the
revolution. They—for instance the problem of management and man and automation—are rooted in what we
call human nature, the complexities of modern production, and the changes in it. As Russian experience proves,
problems of society do not disappear with the exchange
of one dominant elite for another. To transform a social
order resting on gross injustice and inequity is our task,
but such a transformation does not automatically constitute perfection in a revolutionary successor. Ours is a continuing task.

Certainly in 1963 we need not be told that violence, in
the best cause, is no cleansing bath for the souls of men.
Indeed to end the gross violence which has cursed our race
is a socialist goal. There have been men (like Sorel) with
sick, if brilliant minds, who have extolled violence per se
as glorious. The great revolutionists have not agreed with
this theory of violence except as a necessity for the end in
view. Through its purgatory, the road led to an earthly
paradise. Today we have reason to be surer of the purgatory than of the paradise.

I do not write as an absolute pacifist. In the light of
history and the record of the years I have lived, pacifism
seems to me sadly impossible. There have been wars and
revolutions which have advanced mankind, and for which
no better alternative seemed available. However legiti-

mately one should distinguish police action from war or private violence, and police action cannot always be non-violent. Yet we have no scientific right to make that statement so dogmatically as to preclude the possibility of finding alternatives to violence. History is an invaluable teacher, but her lessons are by no means crystal clear, nor are her precedents rigidly mandatory on the present or the future.

Even the physical sciences today deal with high probability or with a limited working certainty. Scientists today doubt that our knowledge about natural forces and their operation enables us infallibly to read the future from the present. How much more true is this in the field of social science. We cannot do laboratory tests in history, or repeat experiments to be certain of the role of each operative cause. We might endlessly debate how freedom would have fared without the French Revolution. Its violence was bred by the oppressions of the old regime. Great Britain, mother of modern capitalism and capitalist imperialism, had no equivalent in violence, nor did the Scandinavian countries. Yet in their democracy, freedom fares at least as well as it does in France. Change came by way of reforms under an expanding democracy. Marx, and more specifically, Engels, admitted the possibility of peaceful revolution in some countries, even if generally violence was to be the midwife of revolution. (More frequently, it has been simply the mother of more violence.)

Within this century, revolutions have indeed risen out of wars between nations and have prolonged suffering. Lenin would probably have died in exile but for World War I and Russia's catastrophic defeat. It was followed by one type of nondemocratic socialist revolution. But total defeat in Germany and costly victory in Italy—without great glory to her arms—led to no democratic or communist version of socialism, but to horrible nazi and fascist revolutions.

The second world war in Western Europe, including Germany, was followed by a revival of modified capitalism, not by socialist revolution, violent or peaceful. I had hoped for a peaceful, socialist revolution. Far more violent social revolution than Cuba's may well occur in many of the poorer, badly exploited nations—without the background of a foreign war. But in the stronger, richer nations, especially the U.S., it would take catastrophe or near-catastrophe, destruction in war, or a worse depression than in the thirties, to make the people willing to risk the pains of violent revolution in order to change its own dominant elite for a revolutionary governing class or group. If history has proved anything, it has proved that sudden, violent revolutions require—or produce—a sterner, crueler, more dictatorial elite than exists in our welfare state, or even under our military-industrial complex. History is written, and public opinion is made, not by the fallen, but by the survivors of great crises. I have acknowledged my surprise at Russian elan after the tyranny of Stalin, but I doubt if survivors of it would have supported the communist revolution in Russia had they had any choice and any foreknowledge of its cost. Only the breakdown in war of Tsarist tyranny made communism's victory possible.

American socialists, charged with advocating revolutionary violence, have long insisted that violence would be introduced only—if at all—by opponents of a socialist government victorious at the polls. The victory we want is

genuinely revolutionary in its economic and political requirements. This we must not lose from sight. Our own
inspiration, our reason for existence, is a desire for a
change in our way of life which will be more than the sum
of successive reforms. Indeed it requires more than can
ever be brought about simply by ballots or bullets. It requires a victory within ourselves of the desire and capacity
for peace, freedom, cooperation; a desire for economic
order geared to production for use and an equable sharing
of what is produced.

It is not enough to blame our slow progress toward
these goals on the owning class or the dominant elite and
their self-interest. It is true that they have a degree of control over communication, education and public opinion
that must be fought. The struggle is made more difficult
and more acute by the power of the military-industrial
complex, which has accurately been described by a recent
journalist as a juggernaut.

But the effort to overcome those dominant forces, and
the system through which they hold such power, will not
be furthered by such loud talk of social *revolution,* as
would conjure up in the mind of the listener visions of a
coming Armageddon. There is a practical reason why the
effort of many groups to use Gandhian tactics of non-
violent resistance is so valuable. We have especial reason
to rejoice that our Negro fellow citizens under leadership
of men like Martin Luther King are using these methods.

X.

Socialism Needs
New Answers

WE HAVE ALREADY observed the fact that public
ownership, or indeed any theoretical abolition of class
conflict between owners and workers, will still leave us
with many actual or incipient conflicts between management and men. The reasons are deep-rooted in human
psychology. It is a problem that is or should be alleviated
by the right sort of public ownership; by the right of collective bargaining, and, in general, by the extension of
democracy in industry. There has been progress over the
old days. But, I repeat, in British socialized coal mines and
railroads, management is still management, and workers
are still workers. They, the workers, are not overly impressed by being, as citizens, part owners of the industries
in which they work—but they don't want private ownership back.

Democratic socialists have usually felt that the first vital
step in the democratization of industry is the recognition
of self-governed labor unions and of the right of collective

bargaining. There was a time when the individual worker
—often an immigrant—had nothing to offer but his life in
bargaining with the collective owners for the jobs and machines without which his muscle and intelligence were
impotent. Today, even labor's critics must acknowledge
the important gains made in these areas of the workers'
existence. One need only to have lived and worked with
the growing labor movement during the years of my political activity to appreciate the human values in what has
been won. But successful social reorganization has not
greatly advanced.

Well-organized industries have won fairly high wage
scales, many fringe benefits, and collective financial re-
serves of a size to make the unions, collectively, a very
great capitalist force by virtue of their investments. But
they have not yet collectively utilized their investments
to attain an industrial democracy. Certainly individual
unionists are scarcely partners or citizens in the industries
in which they work, nor in America, do they show any
great desire to be.

When I was in Germany in 1951, there was among socialists and labor leaders, a real interest in co-determinism,
i.e., the right of workers to be represented on boards of
directors. In some great industries that right was won;
present opinion holds that this victory of industrial democracy was largely ephemeral. Too often, it is said, the
worker-directors become, themselves, bourgeois. So far,
at least, the right of co-determinism has not been much
sought after in America.

Students of the question will tell you that it is hard to
get workers to feel any interest in a job on an assembly
line, or any other job that keeps them monotonously em-

ployed by repetitive tasks, beyond its monetary return.
Unlike craftsmen, they lack the satisfactions in a completed task and hence any great interest in the industry in
which, ideally, they should function as citizens. This is
true: I remember painfully my own summer's work at such
a job during my student years. Yet, the U.A.W. certainly
compares favorably with, let us say, the Plumbers Union,
and, if members of the latter get satisfaction in a non-
assembly line repair job well done, it is not always evident
to us, their clients.

The truth is that to work at democracy either in politics
or industry bores most of us. We like democracy when we
can use it or its institutions to advance some especial interest, or "to throw out the rascals" when we become sufficiently angry at whatever elite is in control. Obviously,
workers who are unconcerned about democracy and high
standards of integrity in their own unions are hardly qualified to be of much use in governing the industries in which
they work. As I wrote in discussing Marxism, their present motto—with some important exceptions—is simply
"more," and many of them are tolerant of the undemocratic and unethical bureaucracies which run them, so
long as the leaders, as one worker told me, "bring home
the bacon." There is less room for a dissenter in the average union than in the civil community.

This is one reason why the positive syndicalist program
of the Socialist Labor Party, which would abolish the state
and turn its necessary functions over to one big union
(Marxist, of course, after the interpretation of Daniel De
Leon), is fantastic. In a country where the percentage of
organized workers is declining, and the quality of their internal democracy is no higher, government by labor unions

has no appeal. Indeed even if the unions were more nearly perfect their function is not to take over the power of the state any more than it is the proper function of the state to run labor unions. Freedom demands pluralism of power and is crushed by too great Bigness.

How big is too big is not a question to be answered with Senator Barry Goldwater's absolutism. In the light of history, the Senator makes his case ridiculous when he declares his willingness always to support better and bigger appropriations for the military and to find danger of freedom's death only in big industry-wide unions, and greater Federal concern for the basic rights of Americans in Mississippi, or elsewhere, to civil liberties, health and education. Empires have been built mostly by arms. And Mr. Goldwater is in favor of more and more expenditures for arms by a government which he seems to think paves the road to hell through Federal appropriations for health, education and welfare.

This whole question of democracy in industry, theoretically so dear to socialists, needs far more study, and far more indoctrination of labor and of society as a whole. Perhaps something can be learned from the Yugoslav workers councils whose degree of control has lately been lessened by Tito in the interest of more efficient production. We can say that the existence of free labor unions is basic and that greater internal democracy and freedom from racism is imperative. I still believe that there is a strong case for direct worker representation (and in some cases direct consumer representation) in the control of great industries. This would certainly apply in the case of socialized industries.

It goes without saying that basic missionary work for

socialism in politics and industry is necessary if any desirable progress is to be made. I find some rays of hope in labor's interest in the New Democratic Party in Canada. That interest may spread in Canada and from Canada to the U.S.

One of our own difficulties is the workers' fear that the right to strike, a right which they cherish as their principal tool or weapon in their struggle for *more,* would be lost in a socialist state. On the contrary, however, this is a right we socialists would protect. Not, as I came near to believing in days of labor's great struggle to organize, because "the workers are always right," but because the right to strike is labor's chief weapon in an economic system wherein the lone worker has only his muscle and brains with which to bargain against the owners of tools and jobs. Collective bargaining is scarcely meaningful without that right. The fact that it may be abused does not warrant its general abrogation, which in itself might summon workers to far more violent acts of protest. Even in a socialist economy, the right to strike ought to exist, although socialist co-operation would have failed to the degree that it was used.

The widespread fear of workers that public ownership would mean denial of the right to strike against state enterprises is not altogether groundless. New York State's Condon-Wadlin Act does just that. The workers are not greatly reassured when they are reminded that no mayor or governor of New York State has rigidly enforced the Act. Our socialist insistence that the state, even the socialist state, is not sacrosanct and that workers should have the same right to strike against a public as against a private authority, gets little heed. If the right to strike in any industry or service is to be limited or abolished, it must be on the basis that the strike would cause irreparable damage to the public as the result of even a temporary suspension of business activities. For instance, it would be worse for the Consolidated Edison employees to strike so completely as to cut off electricity in New York, than for the employees of the public authority, the New York City Transit Authority, to strike. Yet the former do not fall under the Condon-Wadlin Act.

It is part of living in our tremendously interconnected society that certain facilities must be kept going and that in a struggle, neither the right to lock out workers nor the right to strike can be absolute. How to carry out that principle is difficult, but in the case of any limitation or denial of the right to strike in certain industries or services, there must be compensation in collective bargaining and assurance that salaries and wages will not be allowed to fall below those in roughly corresponding lines of work in which such special limitations do not exist. Where socialism ought to help is in the elimination of private profit in these vital services and in establishing institutions and a public climate which will abate the conflicts between consumers and worker-producers, and between management and men. It is a challenging task.

I had written these paragraphs before the long dock strike and the longer newspaper strikes of early 1963 which seriously inconvenienced and hurt the public and discredited the whole business of collective bargaining. The public was justifiably concerned, but hard put for a solution of the problem on terms consistent both with democratic ideals and the practicalities of the situation. Each side, employers and unions, might consider new legislation further restricting the freedom of the other in strike situations, but not their own. Both groups dislike compulsory arbitration and, as a general principle, "government intervention" in collective bargaining. Repeatedly, they have had to accept it because of their own inability or unwillingness to come to a mutually satisfactory agreement. One or both sides have yielded to pressure, but not promptly or with what appeared to be a decent regard for the public interest.

Their attitude invites new legislation. To an unfair degree, public criticism falls almost always on the unions involved in these protracted strikes, but it strains truth to argue that the unions have never used their great power to get what they demand, no matter who or what is hurt. We are no longer talking about strikes against sweatshop wages and conditions, or against the right to organize. (I have been several times arrested for trying to help in such strikes.)

Walter Reuther, president of the United Automobile Workers, proposed, among other remedies, committees of representatives of the public who would act as observers and reporters in the whole process of contract negotiation. He believes in the power of informed public opinion, without coercion.

Senator Javits of New York believes that in certain essential industries and services, the government should have legal right, under carefully specified conditions and as a last resort, to take over the strikebound facilities until agreement is reached. The workers would be required to return during this period of disagreement.

No perfect solution seems to me to be in sight, but the whole situation will worsen if either employees or unions take the position: this is a private quarrel which is none of the public's business. Elimination of private profit in basic industries and services ought to give a better basis and atmosphere for settlement. Government or a government authority as employer, neither here nor in Russia, is the perfect answer to the dream of workers with hand and brain.* There will probably have to be more law, but its values will largely depend on its ability to encourage better understanding between management and labor and the consuming public.

Settlement of labor contracts is made more difficult by evidences of built-in unemployment, even in times of general prosperity. One reason, but not the only one, is the growth of automation. This presents more of a problem than did the coming of the machine age. At first, that also brought unemployment to craftsmen and later to small scale farmers. But it soon created an industrial boom, and thus a demand for more workers. Despite the recurring depressions the maw of industry drew in children and women and forced on the laborers a tragically long day. Marx had some reason to believe that the productive system of his time would mean drawing middle-class folk down to the ranks of the industrial proletariat. He could not foresee how extraordinarily automatic machines could be made to serve not, as it were, as extensions of human hands and brains, but as replacements for them.

Today fear of wholesale unemployment as a result of automation lies behind some of our most severe strikes. Yet automation is enormously lightening the burden of back-breaking manual labor, which men have long believed was part of the curse that fell on Adam. Socialism

* Especially not in the newspaper business; the government must not own the press if there is to be freedom.

would certainly impose no ban on automation. It would
insist that its introduction be planned and that facilities
for the retraining of workers be increased and improved.
It is a bit of a shock to socialists and other thoughtful observers of the current situation in industry that greater
numbers of young Americans are not responding to the
obvious fact that automation and other of our breathtaking performances will require more highly trained
physicists, engineers and technicians. Aaron Levenstein in
his fine book, *Why People Work,* writes:

"While we have yet to find the answer to the problem of
the unskilled and semiskilled foot soldiers in the army of
the unemployed, we are already threatened with shortage
of technical and professional personnel. At the beginning of
the 1960s, U.S. Department of Labor statisticians were already warning that work would be left undone for want of
people with the requisite skills. It was estimated that nine
million skilled workers—for example, toolmakers, machinists,
sheet-metal workers, electricians, patternmakers, welders—
plus five million professional and scientific personnel, constitute the basic core of our mass production system. Each
year, some 250,000 of these disappear from the work force
because of retirement or death, but only 100,000 graduates
of apprenticeship and other formal training programs are
available to replace them. The deficit rises by 150,000 workers annually.

"The Federal Labor Department has figured that our
needs in 1965 would be—for *every hundred* we now have in
each of these categories—137 professional and technical
men, 122 managers and officials, 127 clerical and sales personnel, 122 skilled craftsmen."

In the professions there are serious shortages impending. President Kennedy at a press conference pointed out

that, in 1951, our universities graduated 19,600 students in physical science. In 1960, out of a larger university enrollment, they graduated 17,100. In the biological sciences, the showing is worse: in 1951 we had 22,500 students; in 1960 only 16,700. Everybody knows that we are very short of well qualified teachers. Admiral Rickover estimates the shortage at about 140,000.

Such figures do not mean much to workers—usually it is the less well paid, unskilled workers, who are displaced by automation—a matter which we have already discussed. The whole situation presented by automation is radically changing the manner in which great unions of factory workers rise to considerable power. The balance is changed, and the number and nature of the working forces greatly affected.

There are also occurring or impending great changes in the psychology, not only of work, but of the increase of leisure. The so-called Protestant ethic, which pretty well dominated the industrial revolution and the whole 19th century, was quite sure that Satan would find mischief for idle hands to do. We are now confronted with a mass of speculation about leisure and its proper use. We socialists believe that all facilities for a happy and rewarding use of leisure, in the sense of time outside the job, should be increased.

On the face of their demands, the unions want to solve unemployment due, among other causes, to automation and to increase leisure for the members by winning the 30-hour week. That, as I have said, may help. But not if short weeks with time and a half (or more) for overtime, or the opportunity to moonlight, is the goal. I know of one large building in New York which will not be built because the construction workers would be sure to walk off the job—if they ever took it—unless they were assured overtime, which would mean uneconomically high costs. The small union of electricians in New York won a strike settlement on a basis of a 25-hour week at high rates ($4.96 an hour) plus five hours of guaranteed overtime.

The moral of all this is that the interests of workers organized by trades or industries will not automatically dictate a solution of unemployment problems, union democracy, or strikes. There must be a conscious building up of the concept of the general interest in which each man somehow must be given a part. Automation and the economy of abundance are making possible a new ethics of work and leisure. Western Europe may soon pass into the problem of affluence with unemployment which bedevils us in the United States. To face this situation should be the intellectual and practical concern of socialism throughout the world. We must admit a lack of ready-made answers to fit our underlying principles. But we should admit this as one admits a challenge, not a defeat.

XI.

Socialism and Peace

OVERSHADOWING all the problems which we have been discussing so far is the question of whether men will use their extraordinary power over physical forces to destroy themselves. We could not have got thus far in our examination of socialism without reference to this subject, which we must now study in more detail. We have seen that socialism, by its very nature, has been concerned not only with revolutionary violence but with wars between nations. If mankind is to have a future, the supreme issue now is to find alternatives to war.

The problem presents itself in two closely related aspects: (1) the long range problem of a peace of genuine good will among the sons and daughters of earth; (2) the immediate problem, on the way to this richer peace, of coexistence without nuclear war in a world in which each of the great rival sovereign nations makes its missionary ideology a reason for, and justification of, costly cold war. Can this cold war be ended? Unless it can, there will be neither ultimate peace, nor world-wide good will, such as have always been the goals of socialism.

Even without the cold war the problems of peace would

exist between communist and democratic blocs because
the nations of the latter are also, in varying degrees, capitalist. The extraordinary differences of nations, in size,
power, affluence and interests, together with the pressing
problems of the emerging nations (engaged in what Robert Heilbroner calls the "great ascent") would have been
more than enough to breed wars in the pre-Hiroshima
world. That the post-Hiroshima fear of total obliteration
will, of itself, indefinitely prevent nuclear war is doubtful.
We shall have to find courses of action quite different from
the historic pattern of emerging nations if we are to avoid
great violence. This is a problem for a separate chapter.
But it is in order to mention it here because of its bearing
on the present cold war between the U.S.A. and the
U.S.S.R.

In this cold war we are twice handicapped in world
opinion: (1) our treatment of the Negro race still dis-
credits our professions of democracy and regard for human
rights; (2) the fact—already cited in discussing communism—that the emerging nations were, until just yester-
day, colonies of white empires of which the greatest (the
British, the French and the Dutch) prided themselves on
being democratic.

The best we Western socialists can say is that both before and after World War II, socialism's record on race
discrimination and colonialism has been much better than
that of any other great party.

Communist claims to anti-imperialism are hypocritical
in view of Russia's performance in Eastern Europe, and of
China's in Tibet. After World War II, the British Labor
Party led the way by liquidating the Empire in a spirit
followed, none too handsomely, by continental socialists.

Nevertheless, socialism has been well committed against classical colonialism and, one has a right to believe, against its reappearance in the guise of economic imperialism.

The American socialist record of opposition to colonialism, or what we used to call imperialism, has been a good one. The record has been good, too, in our opposition to racism at home. But Gene Debs and the socialists of his time were too optimistic in their belief that their propaganda for the brotherhood of workers in a struggle for economic emancipation would, of itself, solve the race problem. Socialists were slow to develop a specific program to fight racial discrimination. (I remember my pained surprise when I was confronted at my first Southern meeting in Atlanta, Georgia, in 1928, by a carefully segregated audience! Not by Party fiat, but by unchallenged custom, the Negroes all went upstairs.)

But our early failure to organize for desegregation have been repaired. Today's socialists—including active Party members—place themselves prominently in the ranks of sit-in strikers, freedom riders, and organizations such as CORE. Organized labor, however, especially on its local levels, is still moving much too slowly toward equality regardless of color. Most unions are, nevertheless, nominally on the right track. A.F.L.-C.I.O. conventions have recently adopted the right sort of resolutions.

It cannot be said, however, that Negroes or whites have considered socialism—still less labor unionism—as a necessary or even practical solution to racial ill-will and discrimination. In the current drive to register—against odds —and to vote, Negroes almost always support either Democratic or Republican candidates. The historically-minded contend that it was thus that women suffragists and Anti-

Saloon Leaguers won their victories. This is how organized labor operates with less success than it desires, but with more, its leaders are sure, than it could obtain through a socialist party. It is for this reason that the N.A.A.C.P.—that invaluable fighter for Negro rights—has always been careful not to risk hurting its cause by putting me, or any other person identified in the public mind primarily as a socialist, upon its platform on important occasions.

I have already praised the Negroes for their comparatively successful, nonviolent struggle against discrimination and exploitation. It must not be forgotten, however, that—quite naturally—white segregationism is now being copied by a considerable and dedicated movement of Black Nationalism. The Black Muslims are seeking control over part of the U.S. to rule and exploit in the manner of the whites. That position is an understandable reaction to the cruelties of the white race, but it is not the way either to peace or to victory for the equality of right. The best way for socialists, and for all men of good will, to prove their desire for equality is to promote integration based on true democracy in politics, in industry—and in our hearts.

All this would be true and would need saying in this book even if there were no problems of peace between nations. But in discussing the latter, we cannot ignore the disadvantage to which discrimination puts us. There is no likely alternative to war which does not include recommending to the world democracy and fair play, by the working example of our actions in our own great nation. It is heartening to find that so much awakening to racial fair play has occurred in the last decade. The same moral sense surely can be aroused for deliverance from slavery to wars, hot or cold. But of themselves, neither the mere ap-

peal to that moral sense, nor the better practice of ethical
democracy will be able to save us. The woman who told
me that all we need is a party with a single platform:
Peace, was sorely mistaken. Peace, even in the sense of
absence from war, must be the end product of policy.

We must begin by a general acceptance of coexistence
—in a world disarmed to police force level—under some
international authority capable progressively of giving us
law in place of war. In today's anarchy of armed nations,
the process must roughly follow the precedents of winning
domestic order and the disappearance of blood feuds
within civil communities.

From the usual questions following my talks to audiences all over the U.S., it would appear that the public
assumes that mutual trust between the great powers forms
a necessary basis of coexistence in a disarmed world. It
goes without saying that the more there is of that sort of
trust, the better for us all. It is something to work for. But
the first ground of hope is not trust of mutual good faith
between governments. That has not characterized the relations of governments when their self-interest was involved. Ask the American Indians about the white man's
treatment of treaties with them. We must begin by trust-
ing the assumption that all peoples and their governments
want to go on living.

In a bomb-ruined world, there can be no victory for
communism, and certainly none for democracy. Even in
the United States, liberty will not walk serenely among
the miserable survivors of a future war as they come out
into a world of the dead and dying; a world in which all
the agencies of civilized life have been utterly destroyed.
There is nothing more romantic than Herman Kahn's no-

tion of relatively rapid recovery after thermonuclear war in which the material and psychological damage would be a matter not of long war but of immediate shock, with none of the facilities of daily civil life left intact. The survivors would envy the dead. It is evident that this is at least as well known to the Russian people, who suffered so greatly in World War II, as to us Americans. Khrushchev has proved himself at least as anxious to avoid nuclear war as Eisenhower or Kennedy. But not one of them can drop his role of defender of cause and country.

Both Kennedy and Khrushchev have to consider not only their relations with each other but with their allies. Communism as we have seen is no monolithic force ready to be led by some communist Napoleon. While I have been working on this book, the conflict between Moscow and Peiping—Khrushchev and Mao—has been getting sharper, one result of which seems to have been a drawing of Tito's right wing Yugoslavia closer to Khrushchev's centrist U.S.S.R. in opposition to the grim and dangerous Chinese version of Leninist orthodoxy. It is anybody's guess whether this fact will make world war more or less likely. Much will depend on the West's handling of issues. Western nations could create a situation in which the rival communist powers might feel compelled to stick together.

But this same West, as this book is being written, is itself far from united. Within the NATO alliance is much bitterness over the disposition of nuclear weapons. The U.S. has felt they should be kept in American hands, on the theory that their dispersal breeds danger. De Gaulle insists on developing bombs for the sake of French grandeur; he is less anxious to build up conventional forces with French contingents in NATO—unless he should be regarded as its

leader. He and his fairly constant partner, Chancellor Ade-
nauer, have thus far squelched every American effort to
find some new approach to the problem of Berlin which
they want to keep as an issue guaranteeing the presence
of U.S. force in Europe. De Gaulle is so cold toward the
United Nations that he joined Russia in refusing to pay
assessments despite the World Court's ruling on the duty
of member nations to pay them. He has kept Britain out
of the Common Market for political as much as for economic reasons. All the Common Market members are also
all members of NATO; all have prospered. But it is to be
feared that the Common Market may become an exclusive club, rather than the nucleus of a United States of
Europe.

While this judgment may be modified for better or for
worse before this book sees the light of day, it will remain
true that the two great military powers confront each
other with something far short of unquestioning support
on policy from their allies. Messrs. Khrushchev and Kennedy face insoluble dilemmas in relation to their allies
within the context of the arms race. Their allies are bound
to demand nuclear weapons or control over them. In this
situation, broadly speaking, European socialist parties
have been at best mild and relatively ineffectual critics of
the foreign policies of their respective countries. They
have not, with a contagious conviction, advanced alternative programs.

So far, the overall policy of the U.S.S.R. is the advancement of communism, while the U.S. is occupied by the
containment of communism. Both sides want to avoid nuclear war. Both sides, or at least their chief leaders, want
general disarmament on their own terms, but think that

while negotiation drags on, their only safety lies in deterrence through balance of terror, which balance they continuously upset by a frantic arms race. They pile test upon test, appropriation upon appropriation. This, in a world wherein, between the two great powers, they possess already enormous power of overkill.

In the United States, powerful political voices cry out that we should not talk containment or disarmament, but rather, "victory," even if that victory may require a costly war. Almost as I was writing these lines, Senator Joseph Clark of Pennsylvania was warning us that should we arrive at an agreement with Russia to stop the tests, the U.S. Senate might not accept it. He spoke as a believer that the calculated risk of stopping tests was infinitely the lesser risk since to continue them means to invite nation after nation to join the nuclear club. Each month that disarmament is postponed makes more formidable the task of keeping new nations from testing. Every test, except those most carefully carried on underground, adds to the radioactive fallout, and hence is an act of war against the world. The spread of nuclear weapons makes war more likely, either by accident or by a madman's design.

Among the more recent substitutes for containment have been suggestions that on limited issues both sides might tacitly or openly agree to fight a nice, old-fashioned war (like World War II) without resorting to nuclear weapons. That must be deemed wholly implausible since both sides have gone in so heavily for nuclear weapons. A little, but only a little, more plausible was Secretary McNamara's idea of a kind of gentleman's agreement to use nuclear weapons only against military objectives. This concept puts a premium on gaining enormous superiority in weap-

ons so that the U.S. could strike down military targets
and yet have enough in reserve to deter the Russians
from retaliating by using whatever *they* had left, on
American cities. We could fight back disastrously. Khrushchev has not accepted this counterforce theory. Such a
theory obviously invites a continuation of the arms race
with ever more powerful bombs, and puts a premium on
pre-emptive war. It makes disarmament unlikely on the
part of nations committed to it, and also an inevitable
prolongation of the arms race.

In *Harper's Magazine* (January, 1963) the British authority and Nobel Laureate, P. M. S. Blackett, urges an
approach to disarmament by reduction of nuclear weapons
to a basis of equality. In this connection, he questions
American military policy in these terms:

> "The first possible cause is the obvious military one—that
> it is an attempt to gain such a nuclear superiority that a
> successful surprise attack on the U.S.S.R. would be possible.
> A successful attack would be one that would reduce the
> Soviet retaliatory blow to negligible proportions. Since I do
> not believe that such a blow is possible, and since I believe
> that President Kennedy does not believe it, I do not think
> that the present rearmament program is a deliberate attempt
> to achieve a decisive counterforce capability.
>
> "The second possibility is that the rearmament program
> is not designed for any defined military role, but is based on
> the view that a great number of nuclear weapons and their
> delivery system are good things to have about, partly for their
> general deterrent effect and partly just 'in case' some military
> use could be found for them. I am reluctant to believe that
> such an able and sophisticated military and scientific staff
> as Mr. Kennedy certainly has would justify such a big in-
> crease of the already great nuclear overhitting capacity by
> such vague arguments.

"The third possibility is that the aim of the rearmament is not essentially a military one, but is intended to force the U.S.S.R. to spend more on armaments and so damage her economically and also politically. To some extent this result may already have been achieved. This policy may avoid serious military danger, but will certainly exacerbate the Cold War, and make disarmament unlikely.

"The fourth possibility is that the nuclear rearmament program represents simply the result of all the political, military, and economic pressures which are exerted on the decision-makers in Washington.

"Paradoxically, this last possibility provides the greatest hope. We know that Mr. McNamara has been taking necessary and successful action to bring the U.S. military more firmly under civilian control. May it not be that, in doing this, he has found it tactically necessary to concede a high level of armaments to the armed services and their supporters? The hope arises from the possibility that the Administration will in the future be strong enough at some stage—one hopes soon—to stop the present rapid rearmament and begin the reduction toward a low enough level to give the maximum chance of successful disarmament negotiations. Whether the Administration will soon acquire the power to make this change will ultimately depend on the support for such a policy that it gets from the American Congress and electorate."

Now, let me call attention to the policy set forth in the Socialist Platform of 1962, published as an appendix. I was one of the authors, especially of the section on foreign policy. We reject the possibility of victory in nuclear war. We accept the absolute necessity of universal disarmament down to a police level, but insist that it is only one of the essential strands of a lifeline to peace—or, to change the figure of speech, only one of four basic essentials for avoiding war and building the more glorious peace of

good will. We have to tackle more or less simultaneously
four major tasks: general disarmament, the strengthening
of the U.N. and its facilities to give us law in place of war;
drastic amelioration of crises, and disengagement from
military commitments leading toward general war; and a
holy, cooperative war against the bitter poverty in which
two-thirds of mankind live. That cooperation need not exclude a peace race between the U.S.A. and the U.S.S.R.

Disarmament is essential. We dare not trust ourselves
or our rulers to quarrel while we are armed with such
weapons. Those economically and professionally interested in keeping up the arms race can be trusted—perhaps
unconsciously—to find or make reasons why it should be
adjudged necessary in a world where there is no peace but
by deterrence or threat of war which some day we must
be in a position to carry out.

I have little to add to our Socialist Platform of 1962 on
the general subject of disarmament. Note especially its
emphasis on the necessity of a program for the transition
from an arms to a peace economy and upon unilateral
initiative.

I am sometimes asked why, if the Party—and I personally—believe that in the nuclear age there can be no
victory in war, we do not urge unilateral disarmament
plus a plan for training our people to resist any would-be
occupying power by organized civil disobedience and
even such guerrilla war as has proved so effective in de-
feating colonialism. Against either of those methods of resistance an invader could not use the weapons which
would destroy what he occupied. Moreover, it is argued
that unilateral disarmament would set off a chain reaction
of disarmament. To this I should reply:

1. The American advocates of unilateral disarmament, mostly pacifist objectors to violence, have not worked out how far they would go. In countries without nuclear armament or with very little, as in Britain, there is some logic in pressing for unilateral nuclear disarmament, partly because they are under the protection of the U.S. which does have the bombs. In America, however, it would be as unrealistic to talk about unilateral nuclear disarmament as it was for the knights of old to fight against those who had gunpowder. Only the most extreme pacifists would deny that police force needs some power of physical coercion both in domestic affairs and in a federal world. Was not the army a necessary guarantee of order and approximate justice in Oxford, Mississippi, in the Meredith case? There is a great legitimate difference between force or violence in support of law, that is between police power and war in a lawless world, but there is no more reason to think that the achievement of law in place of war will be achieved by the total disarmament of one of the most powerful of the nations than that it was so achieved in the relations of families, clans or tribes to each other. I doubt if American unilateral disarmament would be contagious. American initiatives on the way to general disarmament might. They would be evidences of good faith in negotiating.

2. It is by no means likely that world war will be initiated or carried on by one great power for the sole purpose of occupying the other. Either power would be rather likely to prefer to incapacitate or destroy the other so that it could achieve its own ends elsewhere. American readiness for civil disobedience or guerrilla warfare might deter an enemy intent upon occupation but not upon other ag-

gressions in the world. In the militant anarchy of a lawless but interdependent world, a potentially powerful nation, granted that some greater Savonarola could miraculously persuade it to lay down its arms, would pick them up again as the Florentines did their luxuries and vices. Disarmament and world law mutually require each other.

3. My final and strongest reason for rejecting at this time a unilateral disarmament, that my own abhorrence of war and the arms race leads me to desire, is based on my estimate of the present psychology of the American people. Were socialists or peace organizations generally to urge unilateral disarmament the psychological block in public opinion would make it harder, not easier, to get the one thing that may save us: their support of ordered general disarmament under law.

The more reason, then, for socialists in every nation to work more earnestly and imaginatively for general disarmament. In the United States, there is a widespread conviction that the unreasonable, obdurate opposition of the Kremlin to the inspection necessary to effective disarmament or even to the ending of tests, is the sole cause of the stalemate. This opposition is usually taken as proof of the insincerity of Khrushchev in talking a disarmament, which he does not want, in order to lure us into a trap, and thus more easily fulfill his threat to "bury" us. The facts do indeed support the need of inspection for effective disarmament and the difficulty of negotiating with the communists. They by no means reveal a tremendously sincere or imaginative American drive for disarmament.

In the fall of 1955 we rejected, out of hand, a proposal for reduction of conventional forces, first made by France and Britain with our approval, and accepted by the Russians in the spring.

In 1957 at a conference in London we refused to consider a Russian proposal for a two-year moratorium on tests with some sort of inspection then not worked out. We said that no inspection of underground tests could be effective; then to improve our "image," we offered a package proposal including the Russian offer somewhat modified, and several other items requiring more inspection or mutual trust, which we were certain the Russians would then reject.

In November 1962 (when I think there was more sincerity about disarmament in the Administration—but not in Congress—than formerly) the U.S. summarily refused to consider a Swedish proposal to the 17-nation Disarmament Conference in Geneva calling for the appointment of an independent and nonpolitical international commission of scientists to prepare a permanent test-ban treaty based on consideration of all available technical information as to inspection, detection and mutual interests of the contending parties. They might at least authoritatively assess the value of the "little black box" as a discriminating detector of underground shocks, seismic or man-made.

It is generally agreed that there can be no absolute foolproof guarantees that disarmament agreements will be kept. More and more we must hope to support agreements by the growth of such a sense of world citizenship that men would feel obliged (and find it possible) to report what seemed suspicious actions even of their own governments in building missile bases or similar breaches of agreements. International socialism ought to be a great force in creating this sense of world citizenship. It certainly should try to rally the world to a test-ban treaty.

More should be done with regional disarmament as an early step toward general disarmament. The disarmament of Austria has been respected by Moscow, even under the strain of the Hungarian rising when Austria was very hospitable to refugees. The treaty, excluding military experimentation from Antarctica, is working well. But the U.S. has turned a deaf ear to all other suggestions of regional disarmament, including the Rapacki plan for Central Europe.

It is to the good that, at last, the U.S.S.R. and the U.S.A. have put on the table concrete plans for achieving general disarmament by stages. They differ primarily because each power wishes to watch out for its own interest in these stages. Here Professor Blackett's suggestion is valuable, and his argument for it is convincing. He suggests that in reduction by stages, the principle should be to keep the number of defensive weapons even on the way down rather than to reduce them by percentages which would favor the U.S., since the latter starts with the greater number.

This theory is sound only as it applies to stages in a rapid approach toward the goal, and if it is geared toward the goal of genuine, universal disarmament down to a police level, under an international federation.

That federation exists in the U.N. The question is of the adequacy of the U.N. under its present charter. It was formed as a great gamble in the hope that the Big Three—the U.S.A., the U.S.S.R. and the United Kingdom—who were winning the war, could stick together to preserve peace. The Big Three was forced by world political realities to become the Big Five, and to include France and some then unspecified Asian nation. India was not yet independent, Japan was the enemy; only Chiang Kai-shek's China was left. The real power to preserve peace was lodged in the Security Council in which each of these powers had a veto. Almost from the beginning, the gamble failed. Stalin was primarily responsible for breaking up the Big Five and beginning the Cold War. Developments in power made the choice of the Big Five invidious to other nations. Chiang's Taiwan is by no means China.

When the U.S.S.R. absented itself from the Security Council, there could be official action against the Chinese-supported attack of North Korea upon South Korea. When the U.S.A. and the U.S.S.R. happened to agree (each for its own reasons), e.g. in opposing the Anglo-French invasion of Egypt, their power was enough to prevail, no matter what the opinion of their colleagues within the Big Five.

Since the Security Council has been thus stalemated, usually by the use or threat of the Russian veto, it has been necessary to turn matters over to the Assembly wherein a two-thirds majority could take certain limited actions of significance. It is an encouraging marvel that the U.N. under these conditions has done as well as it has. It shows the vigor of internationalism.

But it is impossible under its present charter, without an additional agency, for the U.N. to fulfill its full function as the authority progressively to give us law instead of war, and to be the guarantor of disarmament. This because it so badly represents the real distribution of population and power. For example, the United States and Iceland (pop. 179,000) each has one vote in the Assembly. (The U.S.S.R. has three, credited to the Union of Soviet Socialist Republics, the Byelorussian Soviet Socialist Republic, and the Ukrainian Soviet Socialist Republic.) It is a situation which will increasingly constrain the great powers to elaborate use of the carrot and the stick to get votes on important matters before the Assembly, and, if the issues are important enough, to reject the Assembly's authority.

For this reason, I have long supported, and urged upon my fellow citizens, the general plans for charter revision, carefully worked out by Messrs. Grenville Clark and Louis Sohn, in their book, *World Peace Through World Law.* This, among other changes, would base representation on categories of population, with safeguards in taxation or assessment against pure majority rule by the votes of smaller nations. In the tumult of the years since 1945, neither these nor any other suggestions for revision have seriously been discussed in the U.N. or very widely considered in the forums of public opinion. Such discussion as there is, tends to be in terms of blanket support of the U.N. as is, or something close to blanket opposition to it. International socialism, while supporting the U.N., has contributed little that is constructive.

Now it is evident that the influx of new nations, naturally bent on preserving the one-nation-one-vote principle of juridical equality, will not consent to revision along the lines of the Clark-Sohn plan. Its authors, therefore, have come up with an ingenious proposal under which the U.N. itself, of course, with the consent of its constituent nations, would create a World Disarmament and Development Authority, constituted pretty much as the U.N. itself would have been constituted under the Clark-Sohn revision, which organization would be tied in with the U.N.

If this were a book on disarmament, world federalism, and peace, I should be obliged to discuss this whole matter in detail. Here, having stated the problem and recommended the Clark-Sohn studies, I am concerned to say that socialist parties ought to become far more active leaders than they have been in constructive discussion on the subject of international authority. Merely to believe in the U.N. and to cry (as some of its devotees do) that every problem and crisis affecting peace should be referred to it for settlement, is anything but a realistic road to salvation. The American Senate has not even repealed the Connally reservations under which our government must first give its consent before a case against it can go before the World Court. Will such a Senate ever consent to abolishing or bypassing its veto power in the U.N.? Would the U.S.S.R. or de Gaulle's France, or any other powerful nation? The ultimate goal, as socialists should believe along with Clark and Sohn, is a world in which representatives from each country will not represent the government of that country any more than U.S. Senators represent the state governments. They should represent the people and the people's views on international issues. This is a goal by no means immediately to be achieved, or likely to be achieved at all, under the present charter. Meanwhile, the business of laying the basis for present coexistence, and the growth of a genuine peace of good will, cannot wait. It requires prompt reforms in present international arrangements, under which disarmament may be effective as an alternative to war. The dangerous farce that Chiang represents China must be ended, and every effort made to bring the effective government of the mainland into the U.N. on proper terms.

This problem cannot be evaded by setting up an "Atlantic Union" or a League of Free Nations within the U.N. Such organizations might exacerbate divisions within the U.N., and thus reduce its present influence. There is room within the over-all U.N. for regional federations. A more meaningful Organization of American States in this hemisphere might greatly serve peace in the political as well as the economic sphere. It could develop something like the European Common Market with, one would hope, less of the atmosphere of an exclusive and dominating club than de Gaulle has given the European Common Market.

But this opinion belongs more especially to the discussion of the problems of the emerging nations. Before these problems can be discussed, it is necessary to face the continuing threats to peace by the unresolved crises in which American foreign policy is caught. Obviously, it lies beyond the scope of this book to deal in any detail with these crises, and their changing aspects. But it is in order to consider some principles which socialists should urge in dealing with them, whether in Latin America, Southeast Asia, Berlin or anywhere the crises may become acute.

First, the interdependence of the struggle for disarmament and disengagement from crisis must be emphasized. In a disarmed world, many of our crises—for instance, Berlin—would scarcely be called crises. On the other hand, it is a political and psychological impossibility to achieve substantial progress on disarmament while the Cuban, to say nothing of the Chinese, crisis, remains acute in diplomacy and in the public mind.

Next, we must continually remind ourselves and others

that crises have histories in which our own government
bears much of the burden of responsibility for blundering
or worse. I have referred to some of those blunders in an
earlier chapter. Here I say again that Berlin is a direct
consequence of Roosevelt's insistence that our war aim
be the negative "unconditional surrender" and with the
resultant lack of considered policy in Central Europe so
great that Berlin was left over 100 miles within Russian-
occupied territory.

The Cairo Conference during World War II produced
no program for the Far East. I repeatedly forecast evil
results from this failure.

Behind Castro's communism lies not only the long history of North American economic imperialism and support of complacent dictators, but also the Eisenhower
policy in treatment of the earlier stages of Castro's social
revolution. (It should be remembered that the shockingly
ill-advised Bay of Pigs invasion was crushed not by Russian planes but by American planes which we had pre-
viously furnished Batista.) It is as unfair to demand of
socialists an easy solution of a crisis at its height as it is
for a very sick man to demand a cure from a physician
whose advice he has steadily ignored. We socialists can
honestly point to our programs in both hemispheres
which might have averted the development of the present
crises, or made them far easier to handle.

At the height of crises, nobody may be able to do better
than choose between evils. We must include in our
foreign policy a clear recognition that war may be worse
than the evil it is allegedly designed to correct. More than
that, bombs and other instruments of war have been
proved poor weapons against ideas and the social condi-

tions which foster communism. We must present an alternative which capitalism is loath to offer. I myself or in company with others have recently tried to present alternatives to our government's policies in dealing with China, Berlin, Cuba, and South Vietnam, but they scarcely belong in this book. I am here concerned with underlying principles.

I do not agree with some critics, domestic and foreign, of American foreign policy, who believe that its self-proclaimed righteousness is merely a rationalization of national interests in power and profit. But that element cannot be ignored. In particular, it takes extraordinary self-righteousness to insist that we can aid our allies by surrounding our opponents with innumerable bases and missiles, while at the same time insisting that they are morally prohibited from similarly aiding their friends in this hemisphere because of the sacrosanct Monroe Doctrine. This has been abrogated in effect ever since World War I, when we involved ourselves up to our necks in the affairs of the Eastern Hemisphere, our abstention from which was Monroe's principal justification for his doctrine. The concern of our diplomats should be the support of the Organization of American States, not the application of the Monroe Doctrine. More and more we should look to international adjudication or mediation for peace with justice.

Military "containment" of communism invites a corresponding containment of what we call, often too optimistically, "democracy." It is a game both sides must play around the world until good sense abates crises while we achieve disarmament under a strengthened U.N. The world will scarcely accept one set of rules for us in the cold war, and another for our opponents. This applies to both sides.

It remains to consider the fourth great prerequisite to peace: the holy war against the world's desperate poverty. But first, we must consider the price to our own democracy and freedom which we are now paying by insisting that our salvation depends only on an expanded arms race.

XII.

The Garrison State

FOR SEVERAL YEARS I have felt oppressed by the fact that, even in the improbable event the arms race should indefinitely prevent war, under its pressures we should become more and more, what I have called in speeches and writing, a garrison state. The garrison state is, I argued, an inexorable creation of the Cold War. I hailed President Eisenhower's warning in his farewell message concerning the dangers of the military-industrial complex. (I forgave him for many things he had left unsaid and some that he had said.) The warning is worth quoting.

"In the councils of government, we must guard against the acquisition of unwarranted influence, whether sought or unsought, by the military-industrial complex. The potential for the disastrous rise of misplaced power will exist and will persist. We must never let the weight of this combination endanger our liberties or democratic processes."

This statement, coming from a war hero, a General of the Army, has been discussed far less than it deserves. But in 1962, two reliable journalists, very much at home

183

in Washington, wrote *Seven Days in May,* forecasting an
attempted coup d'etat, engineered by an ambitious military man and politicians because a President had signed
a treaty taking the first steps toward disarmament. I do
not pass on the merits of the book, literary or otherwise,
when I say that it is highly significant that experienced
journalists such as Messrs. Knebel and Bailey should have
written it. Around New Year's, 1963, Senator Joseph Clark
of Pennsylvania expressed his fear that, while the U.S.
might get a treaty on banning tests of nuclear weapons,
his senatorial colleagues would not ratify it. We have
already noted that Senator Barry Goldwater, and other
deplorers of growing Federal power, would go out of their
way to give the Pentagon what it asks. We must reconcile
ourselves to the near certainty that no disarmament treaty
or treaties can be negotiated of which the military will
approve. If it had been possible to negotiate reasonable
treaties, immediately after the shock of World War II and
the first two atomic bombs, the military might have
agreed. But now, all those in military professions, psychologically and in terms of status and power, are disposed,
with subjective honesty, to believe that there is no
peace apart from deterrence through enormous military
strength.

I have commented on certain outward and visible signs
of a drift toward garrison statehood of which our people
are largely unaware or to which they are indifferent so
long as it carries them—as they want to believe—to national security, and, in the process, gives them contracts
and jobs.

On that matter, President Eisenhower told us in the
summer of 1960, in a speech at Ft. McNair, that "national

security," that is, the arms race, is one of the "central facts
of our existence; 10 per cent of our gross national product
is devoted to it; over one-third of our scientists and engineers are engaged in it; half of our research monies are
committed to it; no less than 5,000,000 of our citizens are
directly and wholly involved in its program."

The President did not discuss the dependence of great
corporations on this program for their profits. But in his
Farewell Address, he said:

"Today the solitary inventor, tinkering in his shop, has
been overshadowed by task forces of scientists in labora-
tories and testing fields. In the same fashion, the free university, historically the fountainhead of free ideas and
scientific discovery, has experienced a revolution in the
conduct of research. Partly because of the huge costs involved, a government contract becomes virtually a substitute
for intellectual curiosity.

"For every old blackboard there are now hundreds of new
electronic computers.

"The prospect of domination of the nation's scholars by
Federal employment, project allocations and the power of
money is ever present, and is gravely to be regarded.

"Yet, in holding scientific research and discovery in respect, as we should, we must also be alert to the equal and
opposite danger that public policy could itself become the
captive of a scientific-technological elite."

It is absurd to discuss this economy in Adam Smith's
or Karl Marx's terms. It is the economy of a garrison state,
fortunately possessed of such powers of production that
it can spend, without conspicuous deprivation, these vast
sums on that for which there is no natural correspondence
to human wants and needs. We produce arms that we
hope to God we shall never need to use, on the basis of

military calculations which we accept as revelations from the Great God National Military Security. To that we sacrifice, even in our land of abundance, what we might produce for our schools, hospitals, and homes set in beauty. Millions of workers are persuaded that their jobs depend on arms production. Following are some comparisons of military (bold type) and civilian expenditures compiled by Raymond Wilson of the Friends Committee on National Legislation, at the end of 1960:

A $250,000,000 ICBM base in Omaha, Nebraska.
The Dalles, Oregon dam, 1½ miles long for navigation, power of 1,743,000 kw., irrigation, recreation.

The Naval Weapons Plant, Washington, D.C., with a total value of $104,616,800.
26 new 160-bed hospitals at $4,000,000 each.

The estimated value of the Plant's material inventory as of April 1960 was $142,018,907.
35 new school buildings at $4,000,000.

The estimated cost of the aircraft carrier, Constellation, now under construction, of $275,000,000, not including the fire damage of $75,000,000 on December 19, 1960.
The Depressed Area Development bill vetoed by President Eisenhower on May 13, 1960—$251,000,000.

Four attack submarines at $45,000,000 each.
U.S. foreign donations of agricultural commodities through voluntary agencies in fiscal 1959, $178,699,760.

Two nuclear powered aircraft carriers at $470 million each.
The U.S. government spends on its Public Health Service, including grants to States but excluding Indian health, $977,-962,500.

One Polaris submarine is worth $105,000,000, not including its 16 missiles at $1.1 million each.
Emergency Famine Relief abroad on a government-to-government basis, $107,094,000 including ocean freight of $25 million.

Polaris submarine plus missiles, $122,600,000.
United States Technical Cooperation within Point Four will be $150,000,000 in fiscal 1961.

14 B-52, Model G, aircraft at $8 million each or 8 Atlas ICBMs at $13.7 million per missile including all groundwork, launching pad, etc.
The School Lunch Program of $110,000,000 which involves 14 million children.

The Atomic Energy Commission appropriations (mostly military) of $2,686,560,000 for fiscal 1961.
Total government investments in T.V.A., over a period of 24 years, 1933–57, of $2,041,000,000, including appropriations and bonds but excluding revenue receipts.

If for no other than security reasons these military contracts cannot be submitted to bidders in the open market. They have to go largely to great corporations which may have many sub-contractors. There is much interchange between the captains and generals of industry and arms. Old soldiers seldom die; they fade into corporation jobs.

The politicians are very much in the picture. For the most part, they are judged by what contracts they can bring home to their districts. I repeat that Massachusetts voters were easily persuaded to accept Teddy Kennedy on the basis of his slogan that he could do "more for Massachusetts" in bringing home the bacon than any rival. Why not, considering his connections? Maintaining

a modern garrison state has rich rewards for a great many
people who make or find many rationalizations of profit
in the name of patriotism—and all this is done quite
legally. Even the U.S. Senate was stirred by the enormous
profits made by private corporations in the over stock-
piling of certain allegedly strategic materials.

The economy of the garrison state moves further and
further from genuine free enterprise, but not from guaranteed private profits. This is not primarily or chiefly because of the special immorality of individuals within the
military-industrial complex. Given our garrison state plus
our devotion to private profit, nothing else is to be expected. That is why planning for the transition from the
economy of a cold war to the economy of peace is so
essential to any approach to disarmament. To be effective,
it must in the truest sense, be based on the socialist idea
of planning for the common good of men and nations
living in peace.

Both our economics and our politics are inevitably and
enormously affected by the demands of the military in
the Cold War. Security, with plenty of jobs for makers and
purveyors of arms, and a big military establishment, becomes a basic bipartisan concern. In shaping political
programs at home, to say nothing of foreign policies, the
dominant loyalties so long as the Cold War lasts, will be
to the needs, real or reputed, of the garrison state. One
reason the attempted coup d'etat imagined by the authors
of *Seven Days in May* may never take place may be because no President or Senate will feel strong enough to
resist a military-industrial complex, by signing disarmament treaties. Not when the people accept the military as
a source not only of national security but of their own

security in terms of jobs and contracts. Consciously and subconsciously, existing tendencies to think, or rather, feel, about war in old-fashioned terms of possible victory, will be greatly strengthened by the degree to which all of us are caught up in our daily living by the activities of the military-economic complex and in the political psychology appropriate to it.

Consider in this connection the almost unquestioning acceptance of military conscription by the American people. The supposedly temporary law which was set up was re-enacted with little discussion and without even the changes that some investigators had recommended in 1959. With even shorter public hearings and less Congressional debate, the law was extended in 1963 for four years by almost unanimous vote. There was no public protest, and the A.C.L.U. gave it the approval of silence —except to urge that conscientious objectors to qualify for alternative service need not believe in a Supreme Being. This, in a country to which literally millions came, at least partially, to escape the tyranny of European military conscription. The politicians most vigorous in criticizing the over-centralized nation-state, actively support, or do not oppose, its control over every young man— which control is basic to a garrison state. Not merely must a young man surrender years of his life to obedience to a government which may send him to fight a jungle war in South Vietnam which Congress has never declared, or to push the buttons to destroy indiscriminately millions of his fellowmen—an act which his soul abhors; he must submit to the inevitable military indoctrination which made it so easy for Europe to blunder into World War I. No one can support this kind of control in the name of individual civil liberty—it is not even truly egalitarian; it is part of our sacrifice to the Great God National Military Security, and it is a sacrifice that is far more likely to destroy us than to save us.

The one thing that has aroused fairly effective public opposition to the dictates of the bosses of our garrison state is the drive to put us all in underground shelters. This drive is impractical in an age when it is possible simply to stimulate the multiplication of bigger bombs to blow us out. This shelter drive not only tends to make war more likely by its false reassurance but it has psychological effects upon us, and on our conception of individual dignity and decency, not lightly to be dismissed. I warmly commend a book on this subject: *America in Hiding,* by Arthur I. Waskow and Stanley L. Newman.

In other respects, this worship of military security is inconsistent with the conception of civil liberty as embodied in the First Amendment. The Supreme Court is ahead of popular opinion in support of the rights guaranteed in the First Amendment. Yet, in the name of security, the Court by 5-to-4 decisions has supported grave breaches of personal liberties supposedly guaranteed in the Constitution. Thus, the government of the rockribbed state of New Hampshire was allowed to hold that its security depended upon its power to compel an inoffensive little man, a churchman, sympathetic, it was thought, to communism, to tell who came to his farm for conferences with him during the summer. He called it Fellowship Farm, which smacked of *something*. Now, if he had only called it by the good American word, "Togetherness" Farm, things might have been different. As it was, he landed in jail for a year, because he would not tell the authorities what they undoubtedly already knew: the names of his visitors.

As yet, the garrison state has felt that it had to exact few such absurd sacrifices, but it is already armed with Smith and McCarran Acts, and served by Congressional committees ready to reduce individual liberties of citizens to the level of the rights of soldiers in war. Justice Hugo Black in many recent cases involving civil liberties, spoke out, the newspapers said, as an absolutist defender of the First Amendment and the other guarantees of individual rights. Yet this same great liberal judge, back in World War II, had written an opinion upholding the right of the Federal government in wartime to put the entire Japanese and Japanese-American population on the West Coast in concentration camps in the name of security, as interpreted by him. He clearly does not believe in like power in the time of a mere cold war. But judges and prosecutors will apply the principle in the garrison state of the cold war with the approval of millions of citizens who have accepted the rule of the military-industrial complex. They even accept the performance of that modern inquisition, the House Committee on Un-American Activities.

Against this sort of thing we may win victories from time to time. The military-industrial complex itself is not quite monolithic. Emphatically, the battle for civil liberties must be kept up. But we shall not win the war for individual liberty if we live in a garrison state which is obsessed by a concern for National Military Security. The garrison state inexorably widens the gap between individual and social standards of moral conduct.

Democratic socialists and other lovers of freedom have

not been sufficiently alert in making their fellow citizens aware that while we have manufactured the arms of the age of overkill in the name of our national freedom, we have been steadily and inevitably reducing the land of the Pilgrims' Pride to the status of a great garrison state. We shall thus continue until we come to nuclear war, or turn to lead the nations in the great March toward Peace.

XIII.

Socialism and the Emerging Nations

NOWADAYS non-socialists often say that we have at hand the means of world-wide abundance, and that we can do what our forefathers could not; that is, contradict the age-old saying that "the poor"—yes, the bitterly poor —"ye have always with you." Theoretically that contradiction may be true, but in practice, the obstacles are formidable. Certainly the battle against poverty will require planned birth control, lest the human race on this little planet suffocate itself in over-population. Nor can the problem of poverty be solved simply by diverting the billions of dollars—some 120 of them—we now spend annually on arms to satisfying the wants of the underfed. Much as that sort of expenditure might help, human well being requires that two-thirds of mankind must climb out of the abyss of the soulsearing poverty, not kept barely alive within it. It must be an ascent. We of the more affluent nations can mightily help it; but we cannot pull the hungry majority of the world out of the abyss with-

out their intelligent cooperation. No mere relief can
permanently end their poverty. But think what could be
done with the money saved from the cold war!

This is a problem to which international democratic
socialism is not contributing as much thought and effort
as it ought. The Revolution of Rising Expectations cannot
await the transition through capitalism which, Marx
thought, was the dictate of the historical process. "Workers of the world unite" must be given wider, more comprehensive, and more realistic interpretation than 19th or
early 20th century socialism understood. Robert Heilbroner (in his book, *The Great Ascent*) is almost certainly
right in saying that economic development will come, not
as the culmination of a long process of social evolution,
but as a discontinuous jump from one social system to a
radically dissimilar one. Therefore, he warns, "It is not
only wrong, but dangerously wrong to picture economic
development as a long, invigorating climb from achievement to achievement. . . . It is better imagined as a
gigantic earthquake."

In this situation, two things ought to be clear: First,
the traditional socialist arguments about the injustice of
private possession of natural resources and of the great
means of production, have much the same weight when
the "owners" are rich and well-endowed nations, living
among poor nations. It is an ethical absurdity that the oil
of Arabia does not enrich the Arab people except as
sheikhs and kings dispense some of the immense sums
they acquire from foreign concession-holders, who also
wax wealthy from the exploitation of this natural resource.
International programs for control and development of
natural resources are very much in order. So are programs

for freer trade.

Second, the development of industrially backward nations cannot possibly follow the capitalist pattern of Europe, and still less of America. There isn't time. The frustrated will not wait. The situation of these emerging nations in today's age of nuclear physics and of cold war is not the situation of Europe during the industrial revolution, nor of the U.S. in the 19th and early 20th century. It is potentially tragic nonsense to tell India or Nigeria to do what our forefathers did in this rich, underpopulated land. They cannot be expected to go through the capitalist stage to socialism according to Marx's prescription.

I have read and heard more or less eloquent statements from some of our Indian and African friends, which would seem to qualify what I have said about the nature of the Revolution of Rising Expectations. It is too "Western," too materialistic. What Asian and African nations want, each in its own way, is to develop its own culture based on its own values. The virtues of these cultures are proclaimed mostly by those who do not have to live in the cultural milieus they extoll, by men free from the Indian village or the African bush. We may all hope that in the course of their ascent emerging nations will add new and valuable elements to the culture of our race; in the process, they may be able to avoid some of the unlovely features of the American and Russian varieties of materialist civilization. But that the major concern in the industrially underdeveloped countries is national and economic, rather than "spiritual" is too obvious to need documentation. (After all, Jesus taught his disciples to pray for bread even before forgiveness.) The hungry, ill-clad and ill-housed inevitably yearn for abundance, as portrayed

or misportrayed in American movies. What might have developed in India, or, in time, in Africa, without contact with
the Western Industrial Revolution, makes interesting speculation, but is certainly not pertinent to our times. One way
or another, even agriculture will be largely mechanized.
Impoverished soils will require vast amounts of chemical
fertilizer. The whole process will require much capital—
capital that will be either extorted, as an Indian told me
"out of our own already empty bellies," or will be furnished
by those who now have it. Those who have the capital will
invest it out of hope of profit, but they will invest only a
limited amount, and not nearly to the degree that capital
was invested in 19th century America. First there must be
order, and a substantial investment in roads, training for
administrators, schools and tools for industry and farming.
The whole business will require planning. Think what
proper management and increase of water supplies demands in most of the emerging nations. Planning must be
kept as flexible as possible. In China, the stiff revolutionary planning went wrong, after considerable initial success; in India, planning under a mixed economy has not
raised that country's proportionate share of the world's total income. But in neither country, nor in any other industrially backward nation, can planning be avoided. Even in
advanced European nations, it has been necessary carefully
to plan for free trade within a Common Market, and with
the nations outside it. That planning should be consciously
socialist. Socialism in the sense of state-directed, collectivist economy will be the rule in the emerging nations, but
that sort of vulgar socialist economy may easily exist under
fascism or military dictatorship, as well as under the communism which is the object of our national, carefully exag-

gerated fear.

There is one very serious question asked by many students of the emerging nations: will it be possible for these nations to achieve the necessary economic rise under democracy, or at any rate, under our Western parliamentary democracy, which—we are often reminded —is having its own troubles at home. Aaron Levenstein, in his excellent book, *Why People Work,* writes:

"George F. Kennan is quoted as saying: 'If you ask me whether a country—with no highly developed sense of national purpose, with the overwhelming accent of life on personal comfort, with a dearth of public services and a surfeit of privately sold gadgetry, with insufficient discipline . . . has, over the long run, good chances of competing with a purposeful, serious and disciplined society such as that of the Soviet Union, I must say that the answer is No.' "

To this must be added the fact, already noted, that to the great mass of men living under colonialism, the master powers have been those we call democratic. Furthermore, communism has brought very impressive growth in power to a defeated Russia and a chaotic China. Finally there is the unquestioned personal devotion of some communist propagandists. I have heard tales of Indian communists who voluntarily lived with the homeless on the streets of wretched Calcutta. By no means is all of this devoted communist propaganda on such a noble ethical plane.

The average American is much too inclined to think that our main task with the emerging nations or with the older nations of this hemisphere is to keep them from going communist, and that we should give aid on that principle, without too much regard for the kind and qual-

ity of the government we are aiding. Free, let me repeat,
is too often considered a synonym for non-communist.

But there are a great many other disturbers of peace
besides communists. As I am writing this, I suspect that
communism has lost some immediacy of appeal. There
is the matter of the Berlin Wall; North Korea is no show-
piece for communism. The communists are far from
united on tactics, as Mao and Khrushchev have made
very clear. The revolution in Iraq was aided by the
Kremlin against Nasser and the United Arab Republic,
but Kassem's unadmirable government—now overthrown
—did not go communist. Neither have the new African
nations. African students left communist Bulgaria in high
dudgeon.

Lately there has been some evidence—in Pakistan,
South Korea, and several Latin American countries—that
the military may take on the role of cleaning up corruption
and of planning some welfare for peasants and workers
in the Great Ascent. They may do it for the sake of power,
and perhaps also out of some generous human feeling.
Such governments as they set up may not be quite so tied
to landlords and other economic exploiters as has usually
been the case in history. But the rule of the military will
not be the road to peace and freedom for men.

The chief communist advance in this hemisphere has
been in Cuba. Even if Fidel Castro had not always been
a communist—as I now believe that he was—he would
have been driven into communism by our break with
Cuba. If an ambitious revolutionist felt himself and his
country checked by "Yanqui Imperialism"—economic and
diplomatic—what would be more natural for him than
to turn from Uncle Sam to Uncle Nikita.

Other such cases will arise so long as the cold war lasts, and this should be remembered in any discussion of Latin American affairs. If the miracle should happen, and the arms race between the United States and the Soviet Union should become a peace race, concerned for the defeat of the world's poverty, it would be an inestimable boon to mankind. But even so, both great powers, and indeed any conceivable United Nations, would have to face problems such as these: a dangerous population increase, a consequence, in large part, of an essential and humane success in reducing hunger and improving sanitation and medicine; the necessity of providing capital to ease the pain of extracting it from the empty bellies of the upward bound; the difficulty of transition from an agricultural economy, depending largely on human muscles, to a mechanized economy; and the difficulty and expense of educating populations for making these changes—the results of which they desire, but the processes of which they hardly understand. It compounds all these difficulties when one considers that most Americans expect these things to be done by nations pretty well under the spell of the religion of nationalism, and without a tradition of democratic self-government.

Mr. Heilbroner, in the book to which I have referred, makes uncommonly clear his reasons for believing that the conditions of the Great Ascent do not lead easily into our Western world of parliamentary democracy and free enterprise of the more enlightened capitalist type. He is sure that our presently prevailing democratic capitalism does not offer the model for nations, new or old, which are rising out of their poverty. Their economy must be to a large degree consciously collectivist or socialist. So

far, I emphatically agree. But Mr. Heilbroner also doubts
that it can be democratic socialist. "Capitalism and
democracy are luxuries that no underdeveloped nation
can enjoy." Communism, he believes, has an advantage
because it is prepared "both as ideology and as a practical
political movement" to undertake the revolutionary reorganization of society from which noncommunist governments shrink.

Here, I think—I certainly hope—that Mr. Heilbroner is
a little too positive. His suggestive analysis is indiscriminately applied to all emerging nations, without taking into
consideration individual differences. John Strachey, the
British Labor Party leader and theoretician—a former
communist, or near-communist—gave a brilliant series of
lectures in Singapore in 1961, under the title of "The
Great Awakening, or: From Imperialism to Freedom." *
He questions the infallibility of Lenin's theory of imperialism in the light of developments; suggests that communist
nations may become imperialistic, indeed are now acting
as if they were, Russia in Eastern Europe, and China in
Tibet; says some refreshing and true things in answer to
the charge that America has imperialist ambitions.†

Important in Strachey's thinking is his contention that
India's economic progress under democracy can be compared fairly with China's, under communism. Mr. Strachey defends the West against communist arguments
rather than against Mr. Heilbroner's assertions, but his
arguments tend to lighten the weight of the latter's fears.

---

* Published as a pamphlet by the British magazine, *Encounter.*
† What is called American Imperialism is, I think, in large part, born,
not of an imperial ambition, but of fear of communism, and of some
honest desire to help other nations, and—if possible—make ultimate profit
out of this help.

So, in a modest but important way, does the success of the Peace Corps, which seems to show that the emerging peoples like the American way when it is at its best, and that democratic Americans are at least as capable of establishing friendly relations as communist Russians or Chinese. (The wife of one of our embassy staff members in an African nation told me some amusing stories about a very decent Russian, on his embassy's staff, wrestling with problems in a way the authors of *The Ugly American* would recognize as very American.) At present, I think the tendency in most Asian and African countries is to try, in and out of the U.N., to play for a balance of power between the U.S.A. and the U.S.S.R. In this hemisphere, the Latin American response to Russian-made bases in Cuba little suggested a desire to substitute the colossus of Eurasia for their often-suspect big brother, the colossus of the North.

I find myself wondering whether Mr. Heilbroner's theory of progress by discontinuous jumps may not apply to a jump from colonialism to democracy rather better than from colonial denials of individual freedom to similar denials under their own autocrats. (Is it so much more satisfactory to go to death or prison under someone of one's own blood?) My concern for men engaged in the Great Ascent is not that they will find unsuitable some of our democratic parliamentary machinery, but that they will carry into the ascent old tribal, and former colonial disregards of the basic freedoms without which men, even well-fed men, are less than men. It will be easier to make this mistake because under any social order, respect for the right to know, to utter and to argue freely has always required a struggle. It is a sad outlook if national inde-

pendence should be coupled with a vulgar economic
socialism under tyrannical dictators, not easy to discard.
That is why I applaud Dr. Azikiwe's words when he
was inaugurated Governor-General of newly-independent
Nigeria:

"Representative democracy, as it has been adapted to
Nigeria, is based on the concepts of the rule of law and
respect for individual freedom which have been bequeathed
to us during our political association with Britain. These
notions are the foundations upon which have been built
the pillars of our parliamentary government. Without respect
for the rule of law permeating our political fabric, Nigeria
would degenerate into a dictatorship with its twin relatives
of tyranny and despotism . . . With this concept of the
rule of law, we have inherited the idea of individual freedom which is the sheet-anchor of democratic institutions.
The sanctity of the person, the right of a person to fair and
public trial . . . freedom of thought, freedom of conscience,
the independence of a responsible judiciary, an untarnish-
able public service, these are examples of the basic human
rights which I have sworn today to uphold . . . Representative democracy has been tried in Nigeria and it has worked
successfully. Indeed, the Westminster model of parliamentary government and democracy has been proved by us not
only to be capable of being exported to Africa, but practicable in this part of Africa." *

Those who believe that Dr. Azikiwe is too optimistic
should at least agree that government, even if more authoritarian than parliamentary democracies, must not be
totalitarian. It should respect individual rights and pro-

* Nigeria's troubles since independence seem to spring less from
"democracy" than from the fact that as a colony, and hence as a nation,
it is an agglomeration of markedly different tribes not yet caught up in
national unity.

vide a means for change of personnel without violence.

On one point, which Mr. Heilbroner stresses, I must strongly agree. To put it my own way, neither we Americans nor we international democratic socialists can keep peace or truly advance freedom if we are to consider ourselves crusaders *by military force* for our brand of democratic capitalism or democratic socialism around the world. In doing so, we should jeopardize world peace without establishing true freedom. In the long, or not-so-long, run, we would play into the hands of communism or various national fascisms. Our present guerrilla war in South Vietnam is no pattern to follow. We shall get farther by the quality and timeliness of our aid in meeting human needs. Save under very exceptional circumstances, our concern should be that aid is used to help people and their economic progress rather than as a carrot or club over governments. Even the U.N. must make greater progress in winning acceptance of world-wide justice before it can wisely intervene by force inside nations to correct oppression.

Whatever one's foreboding about democracy in emerging nations, there are certain principles that democratic socialism should struggle to advance:

1. The continual strains on world peace which the Great Ascent involves will be enormously minimized if there is general disarmament under the conditions we have discussed. Think of the money and energy it will release!

2. The problems of emerging nations will be far more easily handled under a strengthened U.N., with world disarmament, than is now possible in an anarchy of armed nations, big and little.

3. American aid even now should be channeled, as far as is politically and practically possible, through the U.N. The U.N. expresses a kind of family cooperation in a great human struggle which is highly preferable, psychologically and practically, to the relation of rich uncle to poor nephews.

4. American military aid should be reduced to a minimum, given only under the most urgent circumstances which it will be the business of disarmament to remove or equably to handle with its own peace force. Much of our present aid is a bribe to existing governments, second-rate stuff to satisfy their pride or to control their own people, and of no use in any general defense of our military security, but possibly an added danger to it by reason of its provocative character.

5. Economic aid should be adequate to the project to which it is directed. Only in emergency should it be for breadbasket type of relief. Honesty and competence in carrying out planned projects should be conditions of aid.

6. So far as possible, specific aid to emerging nations or industrially under-developed nations should be in the context of a continuing effort to make the world an economic unit under conditions of the kind of ownership and management and trade appropriate to a human family of nations, rather than of economic and political sovereignties competing for power and profit. To say this is consistent with national emulation or competition in a peace race for human betterment. Here is a challenge to our best thinking and planning. It will require, among other things, that the present successful European Common Market (and a possible and desirable development of something of the sort by the Organization of American

States in this hemisphere) should ultimately be integrated in a common market of the world. Another challenge to the best thinking and planning democratic socialists can produce.

7. Aid should be given by the U.S. and the U.N. on terms that will make it generally easier to relax the religion of nationalism. That may still have some merit as a stimulus to endeavor, and as an antidote to a new type of imperialism. But the plain truth is that the number and weakness of unfederated nations, for instance in Africa, invites a new imperialism of some sort. Many African leaders, like one with whom I talked, eloquently applauded the forceful integration of the Congo by the U.N. on grounds of economic necessity, which would apply with equal or greater force to their own small nations unless they federate.

8. Mr. Heilbroner concludes that "the price of leadership in world economic development comes home to us as a domestic political challenge—perhaps the supreme domestic political challenge." Part of that challenge is that we make our own democracy work and rid ourselves of the curse of racism! What we used to call domestic and foreign policies are inextricably connected, and we can do far more for democracy versus totalitarianism by example than by giving guns or other bribes to noncommunist rulers.

I do not despair when I consider our progress in racial justice at home, the aid we gave defeated Japan toward recovery, our Marshall Plan, our Peace Corps, and an underlying conscience about our less fortunate sister nations somewhat stronger than our foreign (and domestic) critics may believe. But optimism is not easy.

President Kennedy's Alliance for Progress for this hemisphere looked like a long step in the right direction. It came much later in history than it should have, and it cannot instantly wipe out memories of Yankee exploitation of our Southern neighbors or suspicion based on it. But the slow progress of the Alliance is largely due to a failure in Latin American cooperation of a sort to illustrate the difficulties this chapter has discussed. Broadly speaking, with exceptions, neither socialism nor a generalized political democracy has been able in Latin America to get the kind of basic land and tax reform which is imperative. Wealthy landowners and others may be no worse morally than our own robber barons, but unlike them, they have done little investing in their own countries, preferring to send their booty abroad. Time presses. Most of South America is ripe for fascist or communist revolution, without subversion by Mao, Khrushchev or Castro. The only alternative is a democratic socialism which, alas!, is in most countries rather weak. North America can't keep Latin America "free" by bombs and guns, bestowed indiscriminately on any ruler who swears death to communism.

It will be obvious that the sort of program socialism advocates, or should advocate, is different in spirit and action from a program of foreign aid by the U.S. primarily motivated by a desire to buy the nations into our military camp or at least to keep them out of any other. There is a real and deep sense in which wisely to give foreign aid is essential to our national security, because there can be no true security for a few affluent nations in a sea of the grimly poor. This will be true if the U.S.A. and the U.S.S.R. should come to some agreement for coexistence which would end the present cold war. But even during the cold war it is an insult to the best in the American record, and to the American hope for mankind to propose programs for foreign aid dictated simply by alleged tactical necessities in the cold war. Yet this will be the continuing argument for it unless foreign aid is considered as a great factor in that holy war against hunger, which must be coupled with disarmament, in any triumphant turn toward the peace of good will among men.

XIV.

In Conclusion

IF THE READER should ask me whether I think that the democratic socialism I have been discussing has or can at this moment contain answers for all the problems of our troubled world, I should be quick to answer no. It does give many valuable answers and points the way to more. Democratic socialism proposes an economic basis on which other problems can better be solved.

Socialism's primary concern is with economics, the best and fairest way for men in society to satisfy their material needs and wants. In this effort, it has to take account of men as they are, and to consider what they may become. But it can coexist with any philosophy from existentialism or pragmatism to one of the various types of idealism, provided that it does not utterly despair of man's capacity for rationality and decent cooperation with his fellows.

Freud and Adler have not lived in vain. We know that our frustrations and fulfillments are not all in the economic field. Sex is a mighty force in life. Men covet power at least as much as they covet profit, as any comrade in the ranks of the good, enlisted in the service of high causes, can testify. Man will continue under any social system to wrestle with Death and Sin.

I have been rereading Bellamy's *Looking Backward,* by which I was once deeply impressed. Now I know that men could live in his Utopia with far less happiness than he imagines would follow from its admirably just economy. It is more than doubtful that they would or could achieve and maintain that economy of the industrial army as faultlessly as the astonished narrator tells us they have. Men would not fall so easily under its careful regimentation. The government and its bureaucracy would not stay so far in the shadows. It will be a long time before we can have the planning our economic and political life requires without planners—without human beings concerned with power. The elite will not disappear even in a democratic socialist society. Such a society will not be run as one huge town meeting or congress of town meetings. We shall long need leaders; the problem is their selection from a broad base of well educated citizens under democratic controls.

I crave a map of Utopia in my atlas which I cannot draw to my own satisfaction. But I do know that Utopia is not a republic of fraternity to be taken by violence. Neither can it be taken by men who have no vision of better things for mankind. In any foreseeable future, we shall be troubled with the problem of the one in relation to the many, of necessary organization and of the true freedom of the individual. Along with this problem will be the problem of bigness.

In about equal quantities, there comes to my attention literature deploring the size of our present units, governmental and economic, and literature declaring that if we are to be efficient we must deal with urban areas including

suburban and exurban regions far outside the boundaries
of our largest cities. Great is the outcry against the innumerable agencies with some power to tax in areas like Cook
County, Illinois. A well organized urban area could reduce
its bureaucracy and keep a better eye on it. Most of us
would agree that the Federal level of government is more
honest and efficient than most state and local levels. President Kennedy has drawn heavily on Harvard for helpers
whose impact on the badly governed city of Cambridge
was nil. Must we not, then, have more bigness in government?

American socialism frankly cannot provide an automatic
answer to such problems, but socialists at least recognize
them and talk no nonsense about the superiority of private
over government bigness. Great corporations have their
own immoralities and enforce their own conformities
rather more vigorously than democratic states. These problems can be made lighter or heavier by our political and
economic arrangements but they arise out of the nature
of men. The earlier socialist conviction that crime would
disappear with capitalism, and with it our need for courts
and police, is not borne out by psychology or history.

Private crime can be reduced by social justice. To get
rid of slums and unemployment and low wages is not only
good in itself, but in its effect on positive individual development and the diminution of crime. Social justice
makes better men. With all our faults, American life cannot be described in terms of Hobbes' description of the life
of the masses throughout history as poor, nasty, brutish
and short; and we owe that fact not only to our progress in
producing more things, but, under the influence of democracy and socialism, to a somewhat more equitable sharing
of them with a great abatement of government by cruelty.

If you doubt me, read what life used to be like for sailors in the British navy or on the merchant ships or in 19th century sweat shops.

It is an unfortunate fact that if men and women are to work hard for a desirable reform, its blessings must be exaggerated. That has been the history of particular reform movements, as well as of more radical activities. (I remember how woman suffrage was to prevent wars and wipe out corruption, etc. I also remember that I offended a group of good women when I told them that I argued for it on no such basis but on their equality with men in the right to be wrong. I hasten to add that I think woman suffrage has been good for society.)

I shall not stir multitudes, but may persuade my readers when I say that democratic socialism, not sure of all answers, not promising sudden utopias, is the world's best hope, especially if it will more boldly face the problem of war. If we can rid the world of that curse, I am optimist enough to believe that our race can progressively solve the problems we have discussed, while Western man adds to his own glory by the conquest of space.

You ask me if it is likely? I can only answer once more as I have answered before: At this moment if I looked from some distant planet on our struggles as one looks at a horse race, I should be inclined to bet on disaster, the triumph of ignorance, hate and greed. But I am not on a distant star. I have only my life to bet. Somehow, through the ages, we men have won for brotherhood victories which have kept our race alive and moving forward, even when the odds against it were great. Our obliteration, or our social damnation, is not inexorably decreed by fate, not by our gods, not by our genes.

Appendix

I (a) Aims and Tasks of Democratic Socialism
   (b) The World Today . . . The Socialist Perspective

II Platform of Socialist Party, 1962

Appendix I

(a)

AIMS AND TASKS OF DEMOCRATIC SOCIALISM

ADOPTED AT THE FOUNDING CONGRESS OF THE
SOCIALIST INTERNATIONAL AT FRANKFURT, GER-
MANY, JULY, 1951

PREAMBLE

1 – From the nineteenth century onwards, capitalism has developed immense productive forces. It has done so at the cost of excluding the great majority of citizens from influence over production. It put the rights of ownership before the rights of man. It created a new class of wage-earners without property or social rights. It sharpened the struggle between the classes.

Although the world contains resources which could be made to provide a decent life for everyone, capitalism has been incapable of satisfying the elementary needs of the world's population. It proved unable to function without devastating crises and mass unemployment. It produced social insecurity and glaring contrasts between rich and poor. It resorted to imperialistic expansion and colonial exploitation, thus making conflicts between nations and races more bitter. In some countries powerful capitalist groups helped the barbarism of the past to raise its head again in the form of fascism and nazism.

2 – Socialism was born in Europe as a movement of protest against the diseases inherent in capitalist society. Because the wage-earners suffered most from capitalism, socialism first developed as a movement of the wage-earners.

Since then more and more citizens—professional and retailers, artists and scientists—are coming to understand that socialism holds the key to their future. Socialism appeals to all men who believe that the exploitation of man by man must be abolished.

3 – Socialism aims to liberate the peoples from dependence on a minority which owns or controls the means of production. It aims to put economic power in the hands of the people as a whole, and to create a community in which free men work together as equals.

SOCIALISM IN PRACTICE

4 – Socialism has become a major force in world affairs. It has passed from propaganda into practice. In some countries the foundations of a socialist society have already been laid. Here the evils of capitalism are disappearing and the community has developed new vigor. The principles of socialism are proving their worth in action.

5 – In many countries, uncontrolled capitalism is giving place to an economy in which state intervention and collective ownership limit the scope of private capitalists. More people are coming to recognize the need for planning. Social security, free trade unionism and industrial democracy are winning ground.

This development is largely a result of long years of struggle by socialists and trade unionists. Wherever socialism is strong, important steps have been taken towards the creation of a new social order.

6 – In recent years the peoples in the under-developed areas

of the world have been finding socialism a valuable aid in the struggle for national freedom and higher standards of life. Here different forms of democratic socialism are evolving under the pressure of different circumstances. The main enemies of socialism in these areas are parasitical exploitation by indigenous financial oligarchies and colonial exploitation by foreign capitalists.

The socialists fight for political and economic democracy, they seek to raise the standard of living for the masses through land reform and industrialization, the extension of public ownership and the development of producers' and consumers' cooperatives.

7 – Meanwhile, as socialism advances throughout the world, new forces have arisen to threaten the movement towards freedom and social justice. Since the Bolshevik Revolution in Russia, communism has split the international labor movement and has set back the realization of socialism in many countries for decades.

THE COMMUNIST THEOLOGY

8 – Communism falsely claims a share in the socialist tradition. In fact it has distorted that tradition beyond recognition. It has built up a rigid theology which is incompatible with the critical spirit of Marxism.

9 – Where socialists aim to achieve freedom and justice by removing the exploitation which divides men under capitalism, communists seek to sharpen those class divisions only in order to establish the dictatorship of a single party.

10 – International communism is the instrument of a new imperialist state. Wherever it has achieved power it has destroyed freedom or the chance of gaining freedom. It is based on a militarist bureaucracy and a terrorist police. By producing glaring contrasts of wealth and privilege it has created a new class society. Forced labor plays an important part in its economic organization.

11 – Socialism is an international movement which does not demand a rigid uniformity of approach. Whether socialists

build their faith on Marxist or other methods of analyzing society, whether they are inspired by religious or humanitarian principles, they all strive for the same goal—a system of social justice, better living, freedom and world peace.

12 – The progress of science and technical skill, the means to satisfy the needs of man become increasingly abundant. For this reason production cannot be left to the play of economic liberalism but must be planned systematically for human needs. Such planning must respect the rights of the individual personality. Socialism stands for freedom and planning in both national and international affairs.

13 – The achievement of socialism is not inevitable. It demands a personal contribution from all its followers. Unlike the totalitarian way, it does not impose on the people a passive role. On the contrary, it cannot succeed without thoroughgoing and active participation by the people. It is democracy in its highest form.

I. POLITICAL DEMOCRACY

1 – Socialists strive to build a new society in freedom and by democratic means.

2 – Without freedom there can be no socialism. Socialism can be achieved only through democracy. Democracy can be fully realized only through socialism.

3 – Democracy is government of the people, by the people, for the people. It must secure:

a) the right of every human being to a private life, protected from arbitrary invasion by the state.

b) Political liberties like freedom of thought, expression, education, organization, and religion.

c) The representation of the people through free elections, under universal, equal and secret franchise.

d) Government by the majority and respect for the rights of the minority.

e) The equality before the law of all citizens, whatever their birth, sex, language, creed and color.

f) Right to cultural autonomy for groups with their own language.

g) An independent judiciary system; every man must have the right to a public trial before an impartial tribunal by due process of law.

DEFENDS THE RIGHTS OF MAN

4 – Socialists have always fought for the rights of man. The Universal Declaration of the Rights of Man which has been adopted by the General Assembly of the United Nations must be made effective in every country.

5 – Democracy requires the right of more than one party to exist and the right of opposition. But democracy has the right and duty to protect itself against those who exploit its opportunities only in order to destroy it. The defense of political democracy is of vital interest to the people. Its preservation is a condition of realizing social and economic democracy.

6 – Policies based on the protection of capitalist interests cannot develop the strength and unity needed to defend democracy from totalitarian attack. Democracy can only be defended with the active help of the workers, whose fate depends on its survival.

7 – Socialists express their solidarity with all peoples suffering under dictatorship, whether fascist or communist, in their efforts to win freedom.

8 – Every dictatorship, wherever it may be, is a danger to the freedom of all nations and thereby to the peace of the world. Wherever there is unrestrained exploitation of forced labor, whether under private profit or under political dictatorship, there is danger to the living and moral standards of all the people.

II. ECONOMIC DEMOCRACY

1 – Socialism seeks to replace capitalism by a system in which the public interest takes precedence over the interest

of private profit. The immediate economic aims of socialist policy are full employment, higher production, a rising standard of life, social security and a fair distribution of incomes and property.

2 – In order to achieve these ends, production must be placed in the interests of the people as a whole.

Such planning is incompatible with the concentration of economic power in the hands of a few. It requires effective democratic control of the economy.

Democratic socialism therefore stands in sharp contradiction both to capitalist planning and to every form of totalitarian planning; these exclude public control of production and a fair distribution of its results.

3 – Socialist planning can be achieved by various means. The structure of the country concerned must decide the extent of public ownership and the form of planning to apply.

4 – Public ownership can take the form of the nationalization of existing private concerns or the creation of new public concerns, municipal or regional enterprise, consumers' or producers' cooperatives.

These various forms of public ownership should be regarded not as ends in themselves but as means of controlling basic industries and services on which the economic life and welfare of the community depend, of rationalizing inefficient industries or of preventing private monopolies and cartels from exploiting the public.

5 – Socialist planning does not presuppose public ownership of all the means of production. It is compatible with the existence of private ownership in important fields, for instance in agriculture, handicraft, retail trade and small and middle-sized industries. The state must prevent private owners from abusing their powers. It can and should assist them to contribute towards increased production and well-being within the framework of a planned economy.

TRADE UNIONS A NECESSITY

6 – Trade unions and organizations of producers and consumers are necessary elements in a democratic society; they should never be allowed to degenerate into the tools of a general bureaucracy or into a rigid corporative system. Such economic organizations should participate in shaping general economic policy without usurping the constitutional prerogatives of parliament.

7 – Socialist planning does not mean that all economic decisions are placed in the hands of the Government or central authorities. Economic power should be decentralized wherever this is compatible with the aims of planning.

8 – All citizens should prevent the development of bureaucracy in public and private industry by taking part in the process of production through their organizations or by individual initiative. The workers must be associated democratically with the direction of the industry.

9 – Democratic socialism aims at extending individual freedom on the basis of economic and social security and an increasing prosperity.

III. SOCIAL DEMOCRACY AND
CULTURAL PROGRESS

1 – While the guiding principle of capitalism is private profit, the guiding principle of socialism is the satisfaction of human needs.

2 – Basic human needs must take the first claim on the distribution of the fruits of production; this need not deprive the individual of the incentive to work according to his capacity. Socialists accept as self-evident the individual's right to be rewarded according to his efforts. But they believe that there are other incentives, like pride in work well done, solidarity and team spirit which can be strengthened when men work for the common interest.

3 – Socialism stands not only for basic political rights but also for economic and social rights. Among these are:

The right to work;

The right to medical and maternity benefits;

The right to leisure;

The right to economic security for citizens unable to work because of old age, incapacity or unemployment;

The right of children to welfare, and of the youth to education in accordance with their abilities;

The right to adequate housing.

4 – Socialists strive to abolish all legal, economic and political discriminations between the sexes, between social groups, between town and countryside, between regional and between racial groups.

5 – Socialism means far more than an economic and social system. Economic and social progress have moral value to the extent that they serve to liberate and develop the human personality.

6 – Socialists oppose capitalism not only because it is economically wasteful and because it keeps the masses from their material rights, but above all because it revolts their sense of justice. They oppose totalitarianism in every form because it outrages human dignity.

7 – Socialism fights to liberate men from the fears and anxieties from which all forms of political and economic insecurity are inseparable. This liberation will open the way to the spiritual development of men conscious of their responsibilities and to the cultural evolution of complete personalities. Socialism is a powerful factor in promoting this cultural development.

8 – Socialism seeks to give men the means to raise their cultural standard and foster the creative aspirations of the human spirit. Socialism fosters the creative aspirations of the human spirit and encourages the arts by providing a climate of liberty. The treasures of art and science must be made available to all men.

IV. INTERNATIONAL DEMOCRACY

1 – The socialist movement has been an international movement from the beginning.

2 – Democratic socialism is international because it aims at liberating all men from every form of economic, spiritual and political bondage.

3 – Democratic socialism is international because it recognizes that no nation can solve all its economic and social problems in isolation.

4 – Absolute national sovereignty must be transcended.

5 – The new world society for which socialists strive can develop fruitfully in peace only if it is based on voluntary cooperation between nations. Democracy must, therefore, be established on an international scale under an international rule of law which guarantees national freedom and the rights of man.

6 – Democratic socialism regards the establishment of the United Nations as an important step towards an international community; it demands the strict implementation of the principles of its Charter.

FIGHTS IMPERIALISM

7 – Democratic Socialism rejects every form of imperialism. It fights the oppression or exploitation of any people.

8 – A negative anti-imperialism is not enough. Vast areas of the world suffer from extreme poverty, illiteracy and disease. Poverty in one part of the world is a threat to prosperity in other parts. Poverty is an obstacle to the development of democracy. Democracy, prosperity and peace require a redistribution of the world's wealth and an increase in the productivity of the underdeveloped areas.

All peoples have an interest in raising the material and economic, social and cultural development of these areas unless they are to fall victims to new forms of oppression.

9 – Democratic socialists recognize the maintenance of world peace as the supreme task in our time. Peace can be secured only by a system of collective security. This will create the conditions for international disarmament.

10 – The struggle for the preservation of peace is inseparably bound up with the struggle for freedom. It is the threat to the independence of free peoples which is directly responsible for the danger of war in our time.

> Socialists work for a world of peace and freedom, for a world in which the exploitation and enslavement of men by men and peoples by peoples is unknown, for a world in which the development of the individual personality is the basis for the fruitful development of mankind. They appeal to the solidarity of all working men in the struggle for this great aim.

(b)

THE WORLD TODAY . . .
THE SOCIALIST PERSPECTIVE

ADOPTED AT THE CONGRESS OF THE SOCIALIST
INTERNATIONAL IN OSLO, 1962

The Socialist International consists of 41 member parties. In terms of active membership, they number over $10\frac{3}{4}$ million, but they command the support of nearly 70 million voters. Some are large parties, some are small. Some are parties which lead, or share in government, some are parties in opposition. These parties, fulfilling complex responsibilities and functions, share a common purpose in their membership of the Socialist International and their dedication to the cause of democratic Socialism.

It was in Europe that the social struggle first took on an organised form, in the creation of Socialist and Labour Parties. It is in Europe that democratic Socialists have marked their finest achievements and where their greatest power resides. Both at home and abroad, they championed political freedom and social justice.

The voice of democratic Socialism is heard in Asia, in Africa and in Latin America. In Asia, the Socialist International has friendly relations with parties in the Asian Socialist Conference. Early in 1962 the Socialist International sent a Mission which received a warm welcome in the new countries of Africa and which has marked out a field of immediate common activity. In 1963 a Mission is touring Latin America where the influence of democratic Socialism over recent years has contributed to the downfall of dictatorships, but where the definition of new tasks in the turbulent political arenas of these countries still awaits completion.

In joining the Socialist International, parties retain their autonomy but extend their political influence. At Congresses of the Socialist International they meet to define their attitudes to major issues confronting the world. The International aims to unite into effective membership all those parties which aim at the realisation of the principles of democratic Socialism. The Congress elects an executive body, the Bureau, to conduct its affairs between its sessions.

The Socialist International provides the channel for counsel and mutual help between its member parties. It co-ordinates their activities and keeps them informed about what each other is doing.

The Socialist International fights against totalitarianism, against imperialism, and against exploitation in all its forms. Its member parties are united in their aim to establish for all mankind a world of peace with freedom and social justice.

The Socialist International reaffirms the principles of the Frankfort Declaration of 1951 on the 'Aims and Tasks of Democratic Socialism.'

In the 'fifties, it became apparent that the many new scientific discoveries, if applied for peaceful purposes, made possible for the first time in history the elimination of hunger and poverty from the face of the earth. The same discoveries, used for military purposes, could cause the end of our civilisation.

There are few decades in history which have produced such vast and varied changes. The work which Socialist governments began of responding to the urge for independence among colonial peoples was carried forward. By 1960, most countries of Asia and Africa had won their independence and joined the concert of free nations. Thus, for the first time in history, peoples of all continents meet together freed from alien domination. The Socialist International greets the thousand million people of the new States and welcomes their participation in the common quest for justice, equality and peace for all mankind.

Nevertheless, colonialism still survives. It is significantly entrenched in countries where no Socialist movement has been allowed to exist and where democracy itself has been suppressed. The Socialist International finds no moral justification for the continued existence of colonialism and condemns it in all its forms.

In many democratic countries in the past decade, economic expansion enabled striking progress to be made towards the welfare society, and consequently the age-old insecurities of their citizens were substantially reduced. Yet at the same time, the gap in the standard of living between rich and poor nations has widened still further. Hundreds of millions still suffer from hunger and poverty.

In the 'fifties, the will of the human spirit for freedom and dignity was repeatedly asserted. In many countries of Latin America, dictatorships were overthrown. In some parts of the Communist world, the iron grip of Stalinism was weakened. Stalin himself was condemned. The proclamation of destalinisation was prompted by popular pressure to break with the detested past and to initiate new policies. But the brutal repression of freedom in the Communist world and the ceaseless efforts of Communism to extend its sphere of influence continue.

In the decade that is over, the world faced many crises. In some parts of the world, armed conflict broke out. However, the deep-seated hostility to war that characterises peoples everywhere helped to avert world war.

SOCIALISM AND INDUSTRIALISED COUNTRIES

The most dynamic impulse towards social change has come in countries where democratic Socialist parties have been able to exert effective influence. History has not confirmed the doctrine of the increasing misery of the proletariat. The worst excesses of capitalism have been corrected through the constant activity of the Socialist parties, the trade unions and the co-operative societies. New forms of ownership and control of production have emerged. Mass unemployment has been eliminated, social security extended, working hours have been reduced and educational and vocational opportunities widened.

Even where democratic Socialists have been in opposition, their opponents have often been obliged by public opinion to adopt essentially Socialist solutions for the problems of full employment and social welfare. Likewise, in the United States of America, pressures of trade unions and other progressive social forces have made their influence felt.

Despite these improvements, serious problems continue to plague industrialised societies. We believe that they cannot be solved without the application of the principles of democratic Socialism.

Permanent control by the State and public institutions over the economy undoubtedly diminishes the danger of the recurrence of economic crises. Nevertheless, recessions, which interrupt steady economic expansion, still continue.

The increasing concentration of economic power and the growth of monopoly when not controlled also create serious problems. The increasing size of industrial undertakings has brought into being a new class of managers, who enjoy great power without being responsible to the community for the manner in which they exercise it. A task facing Socialism is to make this group aware of its social responsibilities.

In many countries, the level of investment, though higher than it was, is still far below what could be achieved in a properly planned economy. Investment is, moreover, frequently wasteful. Too often, it is directed towards immediate capitalist profit, instead of strengthening in a planned fashion the basis of the economy or meeting urgent social and cultural needs.

Notwithstanding the considerable improvement in the standard of living of the mass of the people, gross inequalities in the distribution of wealth and income remain. The greater part of privately-owned wealth is still in the hands of very few. Tax evasion and the immense appreciation of capital values perpetuate this evil. Society is still divided into social classes with differences in status and living standards, based on the accident of birth and inheritance, and resulting in differences in opportunities for education and training. Exaggerated emphasis on purely materialist aims is increased by modern business advertising and by the commercialisation of cultural activity, imposing a trend towards drab conformity.

Democratic Socialism has achieved much, but greater tasks still lie ahead. There is no single method to remedy the evils of present-day society. To achieve a fair distribution of wealth, we require an extension of public ownership and control and other legislation to curb private monopolies, to effect a radical reform of the tax system and to protect consumers.

State action, authorised by democratic decisions, is essential to provide for a rapid rate of economic expansion, a sufficiently high level of investment and the swift application of modern scientific techniques. This involves economic and social planning as a central government responsibility.

In democracy, a framework must be created within which the workers can effectively influence decisions and conditions in industry and the economy generally.

The democracies must improve and extend the techniques which will enable them to direct their economic resources so as to serve the long-term interests of the people and to facilitate a more substantial contribution to world economic development. They have yet to establish sufficiently close co-operation with one another to assist the steady development of international trade, unimpeded by high tariff barriers and undisturbed by exchange and currency crises. Economic planning outgrows the borders of national States. The establishment of regional economic organisations is a recognition of this fact.

The free development of the human personality can be ensured only by a reform of the existing social and economic structure. For those still living in poverty, improvement of conditions must be realised by a system of fair wages and of effective social security and family allowances and individual care and help. A basic requirement is the provision of a general system of education with a truly democratic character and ensuring genuine equality of opportunity for all. Education in citizenship, vital to democracy, should be promoted both by the State, and by voluntary organisations, such as political parties, trade unions, co-operatives and educational associations.

Democracy can hope for survival only if it can base itself on the keen interest and active participation of citizens in its functioning. The democratic process can be extended and deepened through territorial decentralisation and industrial democracy. Press, radio and television, free from undemocratic controls and pressures, should provide ample opportunities for free, responsible debates on political issues.

The challenge of the generation that inherited the changed society of the 'sixties is to find the ways and means of completing the task begun. To meet this challenge, this generation must direct its ingenuity and energy to the world as a whole.

SOCIALISM AND EMERGENT NATIONS

The emergent nations, with their hundreds of millions of people, have a heavy burden of poverty to overcome. Their difficult task is an exciting one because independence has released great reservoirs of vitality. There should be available to the new States the whole stock of science, technology and political experience that has been accumulated by the developed countries.

These new States have the opportunity of escaping the evils of Capitalism and Communism alike. The capitalist methods of ruthless exploitation of the workers, involving the uprooting of the peasants and driving them into urban slums, are not only obnoxious, but also unnecessary. The Communist method is equally obsolete, consisting as it does of abstracting surplus value through terror and undertaking break-neck industrialisation by the sacrifice of the needs of the people and more particularly at the cost of agricultural development.

The future belongs no more to Communism than to Capitalism. Communism and Capitalism point back to an age where human beings were treated as raw materials and not as the source and objective of all efforts. The Socialist International greets with satisfaction the fact that so many of the new States, striving to plan their economic future, are inspired by the ideas of democracy and Socialism.

The new States have the opportunity to plan their economy, combining agriculture with industry, reviving agriculture through improved peasant farming and co-operative organisation. Better distribution of industries and decentralisation of the productive process can obviate the growth of new urban conglomerations. The new States which began their industrial journey not with steam power but with electricity, have greater freedom to plan their development.

The emergent nations, with the co-operation of the developed countries, can avoid many conflicts such as those between urban and rural populations. The new nations suffer from stagnant economic conditions and an ossified social structure. Balanced development depends on releasing and co-ordinating the forces of individual and economic initiative, without allowing private enterprise to reap the profits for the enrichment of a small minority. Fair play and fair shares must now become the basis of their policy.

These possibilities can be fully realised only if the new States pay due attention to the spread of education, for children as well as adults, to the diffusion of skills and general knowledge among the people and to helping families to plan their growth.

The future of emergent nations in this age of transition depends on the efforts of Socialists and other democratic progressive forces in new nations and on aid from the developed countries. The need is greatest in training, in the provision of skilled technicians and in the accumulation of investment capital. Industrialised countries should provide at least 1 per cent of their national income for grant aid programmes. It should be the consistent policy of the Socialist International to unite the Socialist forces of all countries in the great endeavour of accelerating the progress of the new States.

The Socialist International recognises the right of all nations to self-determination. Nationalism has often been a liberating and uplifting force, but when it is taken to extremes, it can threaten human freedom and progress. The dangers of nationalistic excesses, where the welfare of the people is sacrificed to the claims of the State, can be averted if, on the one hand, the Socialists in the richer countries succeed in raising the sights of their people above their national needs, and, on the other hand, Socialists in the new countries develop their economy in such a way that the yardstick is human welfare and not national prestige.

There is the danger that the people of new States will be lured by the false perspectives of authoritarianism. Recent experience in Europe, in Asia, in Africa, in Latin America shows how barren this repudiation of democracy can be.

The countries of Latin America, although long free from colonial rule, share some of the problems of emergent nations. Here, scores of millions of people also present democratic Socialism with the insistent problems of hunger, illiteracy and disease.

The developing countries face a tremendous task of trans-

formation involving basic reorientation of the rhythms of life
and work of their people. The Socialist International recognises that these far-ranging changes in patterns of thought
and behaviour among hundreds of millions of people cannot
be brought about unless the developed countries also undertake some fundamental adjustments in their patterns of
thought and action. To that pioneering task of social innova-
tion and adjustment, the Socialist International will dedicate
its main efforts.

SOCIALISM AND THE COMMUNIST COUNTRIES

Substantial economic expansion in the Soviet Union has led
to improved living standards but, above all, to greater military
potential. In China, industrialisation is advancing. The fact
that the formidable power of a State containing 600 million
people is subject to totalitarian rule and severe discipline,
cannot be ignored. It presents a threat to other Asian countries.
Industrialisation and modernisation at the tempo at which
they are realised in the Communist sphere are maintained
only at the cost either of preventing the essential freedoms
from developing or destroying them where they are already
in existence.

In the case of Russia this was accompanied, especially in
the earlier part of the decade, by ruthless exploitation of the
countries of Eastern Europe. The risings of the people in East
Germany, Poland and Hungary, who showed such dauntless
courage against overwhelming odds, were in part provoked
by these policies. Although the revolts were suppressed, they
forced the Soviet leaders to make concessions. However, the
Soviet Union strives to retain political control over the
countries of Eastern Europe. The ban on the activities of
the Socialist parties in these countries has continued, though
their ideals and traditions have been kept alive in the minds
and hearts of countless supporters.

The Communist world is no longer led from one centre of
power. The Russian and Chinese leaders differ on essential
issues of policy. Their divergent interests lead to a clash of

ideology. This is the most important open breach so far in the structure of the Communist bloc.

Despite opposition from the Chinese Communists, the Soviet leaders abandoned the theory of an inevitable war between Capitalism and Communism. As a consequence, they now claim to base their foreign policy on the principle of peaceful co-existence. In practice, however, this is only a change of tactics, and the struggle against the non-Communist world is continued in a different form. The Communists admit that the conflict is not diminished, but the emphasis merely shifted from the purely political to the economic, social and ideological fields.

Communism is not merely a social, political and economic system, but a set of doctrines which its advocates claim to be infallible and which they strive to extend all over the world.

Rivalries in the Communist sphere between different centres of Communist power and currents of opinion concerning Communism, make it manifest that Communist pretensions to totalitarian control over the individual, the nation and the development of society, are incompatible with the nature of man, the role of the nation and the evolution of human society.

For Communists, the end justifies the means, and there is a permanent contradiction between what they say and do.

Although the Communist countries claim to be peace-loving, the way in which they have used their military power has aggravated tension in the world. Although they encourage the non-aligned countries when they can exploit the attitude of the latter in their own favour, they condemn them when they cannot.

Although the Communist countries use the strongest anti-colonial language, they have enslaved scores of millions of people.

Misusing the word Socialism, their one-party dictatorships represent in fact tyranny, denying those freedoms of speech, religion, criticism, voluntary organisation and contacts with the outside world which are the essence of a democratic society.

SOCIALISM AND WORLD PEACE

The ultimate objective of the parties of the Socialist International is nothing less than world government. As a first step towards it, they seek to strengthen the United Nations so that it may become more and more effective as an instrument for maintaining peace. Nations should settle their disputes peacefully, without resort to force. The Charter of the United Nations and the decisions based on it should be respected by all. Its constitution and structure must reflect the increasingly important role which the new countries play on the world scene. Membership of the United Nations must be made universal, so that all nations, including China, may be represented by their governments in power.

We deny that the world is forever destined to be polarised into blocs. Our constant endeavour is to put an end to the cold war. East-West rivalry has largely been imposed upon an unwilling world by the Communist leaders. In Asia tensions have been aggravated by Chinese actions in North India and elsewhere, but also by some aspects of American policy. This rivalry is dangerous. It diverts energies from constructive tasks. To democratic Socialists co-existence is not enough. International co-operation is the need of our time.

The Socialist International stands for complete disarmament both in nuclear and conventional weapons, including all countries and subject to truly effective controls. We shall never give up the patient search for practical solutions to outstanding disputes between nations.

Democratic Socialists seek nothing but lasting peace, but they will firmly defend their liberties. They therefore reject the idea that democracies should disarm unilaterally. The power of defence in the event of attack must therefore be preserved as a deterrent to aggression.

The United Nations has often helped to resolve disputes between nations. However, it is, in its present form, not in the position to grant protection to a country which is the victim of aggression and to guarantee the security of every country. In these circumstances, each nation must accept responsibility for its own security. Some consider that a non-alignment foreign policy serves the security and the political stability in their own area in the best way. The International respects the desire of nations to be free to pursue their destiny without commitment in power relations of the world. Most of the Western democracies have joined to form the N.A.T.O. Alliance. The democratic Socialist parties in the countries of the Alliance consider this a powerful bulwark of peace and declare their firm determination to uphold it.

While it is vital that the uncommitted countries should not fall under Communist control, no attempt should be made to draw them against their will into the Western alliance. Nor must the opposition to Communism be allowed to develop into support for Fascist, reactionary and feudal regimes. On the contrary, pressure should be continually maintained for the restoration of liberties and for social and economic reforms.

THE SUMMONS OF THE 'SIXTIES

In 1951, we declared in Frankfort:

'Socialists work for a world of peace and freedom, for a world in which the exploitation and enslavement of men by men and peoples by peoples is unknown, for a world in which the development of the individual personality is the basis for the fruitful development of mankind.'

These words sum up our faith.

We now stand at a great divide in history. Man, through his mastery over nature and the maturing of feeling for justice and equality, is struggling to shed the old moulds of work and thought.

We democratic Socialists proclaim our conviction that the ultimate aim of political activity is the fullest development of every human personality, that liberty and democratic self-government are precious rights which must not be surrendered; that every individual is entitled to equal status, consideration and opportunity; that discrimination on grounds of race, colour, nationality, creed or sex must be opposed; that the community must ensure that material resources are used for the common good rather than the enrichment of the few; above all, that freedom and equality and prosperity are not alternatives between which the people must choose but ideals which can be achieved and enjoyed together.

We are determined to build peace not by conquest but by understanding.

We repudiate alike the soulless tyranny of Communism and the wasteful injustice of Capitalism.

To us, both freedom and equality are precious and essential to human happiness. They are the twin pillars upon which the ideal of human brotherhood rests.

In proclaiming once again our faith in that ideal, we know that we speak for humanity everywhere.

The Socialist International calls upon the people of the world, and youth in particular, to seize the opportunities that the efforts of earlier generations have at long last opened up for all, and to continue the struggle for a better world.

Appendix II

PLATFORM OF SOCIALIST PARTY, 1962

The Socialist Party is the organized expression of democratic socialism in the United States. It was founded in 1901. It is the sole U. S. affiliate of the Socialist International, the body to which the major socialist and labor parties of the world belong. Under the leadership of two great Americans, Eugene V. Debs and Norman Thomas, the Socialist Party has made many signal contributions to American life. With the onset of a new period of political soul-searching, many Americans are turning toward democratic socialism as a source of new ideas, inspiration, guidance; and it is to them that we commend this platform. It is our hope that all who share our vision will join with us in building our party into an ever more effective instrument for translating our ideals into living reality.

This platform was adopted at the Socialist Party's national convention held at the Hotel Raleigh in Washington, D.C., on June 8th, 9th and 10th, 1962.

INTRODUCTION

These are times of basic crisis and fundamental decision. Yet, as never before in our national life, there is failure of vision, listlessness of the political and moral imagination.

During the Eisenhower Fifties there was complacency and celebration, and only the barest recognition of the most ob-

vious challenges at home and abroad. In the first two years
of the Kennedy Administration there has been a certain re-
awakening of social conscience, but this has been sporadic,
focused on limited and specific issues, unmindful of the
enormous options facing the world in which we live.

The plain fact is that mankind is in the process of a break-
through more dramatic and profound than the conquest of
outer space; at a turning point more decisive than the transition from stone age to bronze.

We are coming to live in an unprecedented environment.
An entire planet is being made subject to a revolutionary
technology which reshapes men and women as well as things.
Whole populations are about to live under fundamentally new
conditions.

This modern technology is one of the two radical facts of
our time. In the form of nuclear weapons, it holds out the
possibility of an ultimate war, of annihilation at worst and an
incalculable retrogression of civilization at best. Within domestic society, the new technology could become the basis
of the most comprehensive and antihuman tyranny man has
ever known; or it could fulfill the immemorial dream of hu-
mankind for a life of decency and dignity.

The modern technology is social. Domestically it has already
produced an integrated economy. It is creating one world
whether we recognize the fact or not. When power takes on
this character, when it becomes concentrated and all-embrac-
ing, its use can no longer safely be decided by minority elites
acting in their own self-interest. If man is to survive, and if
we are to use our technology for the deepening of freedom,
our only hope lies in the popular assertion of democratic control over the means of production and destruction.

For man is the second radical fact of our time. We will
impart purpose to our new technology; the choice is ours.
It may be that we shall be overwhelmed by the genius of our
own hands, that we are unequal to the challenge of what we
ourselves have made. If so, we will have failed and failed
radically and the consequence of our lack of vision will be

a tragedy dwarfing anything that has happened in human history.

But if we are radical in the best sense of the word, if we master this revolutionary technology rather than being mastered by it, then our hopes can be unbounded.

The gigantic issues of our times are not going to be solved in a day, a year, or a decade. There are no simple blueprints for a transformation as basic as the one which is taking place now. And yet, if we are to make the first tentative and painful advance, if we are to move at all, we must have a vision.

The unique contribution of democratic socialism in these times is not some final and finished program which contains all the answers. Rather, it is a vision which clearly states an ultimate goal and at the same time clarifies and informs immediate proposals.

Given the social character of our new world and the nations composing it, we cannot seek peace, freedom, or plenty by turning back to an imagined golden age of individual entrepreneurs. Neither can we have confidence in corporations or commissars. The most basic stuff of our socialist vision is this: that democracy is not simply a political form, that the extension of democracy to the economy and the society and to the world itself is the only way in which the new technology can be made the servant of man.

In what follows, we will be primarily concerned with the immediate political approximations of this vision. Yet in every word we write there is a sense of the radical character of the times in which we live, of a basic option for peace and freedom through democracy.

DOMESTIC AFFAIRS

At home, America confronts basic crises. Under Eisenhower they were ignored; under Kennedy some of them have been recognized, but piecemeal. What is required transcends this or that reform. What we need is a new point of departure:

democratic social planning.

There is the crisis of automation. Jobs are being destroyed, whole categories of men and women are being rendered obsolete. We have responded to this with passivity and helplessness. We have watched a steady growth of the long-term unemployed, we have seen the reappearance of depression sectors in the society. Ironically, we are now working toward the goal of a 4 per cent rate of unemployment, as if that represented some kind of a utopia.

And the crisis of automation has only begun. Retooling has so far taken place among the obvious jobs, striking at the semi-skilled industrial worker. But in the years to come technology will revolutionize clerical occupations and even the middle levels of management. If it is left uncontrolled and unplanned, "progress" will come as a curse to millions, the great gains of industrial unionism will be eroded, and American society, at the moment of abundance, will become more lopsided and unjust. And as is the case in almost every domestic crisis, the racial minorities will bear the great burden of this tragedy.

There is the crisis of the cities. Less than 10 per cent of the American people now live on farms. The millions are herded into megapolis, the vast urban areas that sprawl for hundreds of miles. By far and large this development is "planned" through real estate speculation without regard for social and individual human values.

As a result, practically every city in the land faces a crisis of traffic congestion, of slums packed more densely than ever before, and of growing cost. For the municipal chaos is expensive in terms of health, police, fire, and welfare protection; and as the middle class flees the central city areas, financial resources for facing the problems decline.

In all of this, Federal intervention tends to be haphazard and uncoordinated. Thus has been produced one of the great scandals of our time: "Socialism for the rich, free enterprise for the poor." In the name of the common good we have subsidized those who have funds to look after themselves; we have shunted the defenseless into ghettoes based on social class and poverty.

Crisis of Social Values

There is a basic crisis of social values in America. Our tremendous resources are allocated not on the basis of human need as democratically determined, but in the quest for profit. On the one hand this produces a society of economic and social distortion which prefers to satisfy the luxuries and pseudo-needs of the rich rather than to deal with the desperate needs of working men and women: millions for pink telephones and auto style-changes, pitifully little for housing. On the other hand it has created huge industries whose purpose is to manipulate people, to convince us through radio and television and the press that we enjoy being exploited for the profit of the few.

There is the most urgent single moral crisis of our land, civil rights. This is not simply a question of striking down the statutes of discrimination. Negroes and other minorities are the victims of economic and social Jim Crow as well as of racist laws. We have institutionalized their victimization by putting them at the bottom of society. To talk of real equality is also to speak of destroying the racial ghettoes (which can only be done by public housing), of a new attitude on automation, of a different view of the society as a whole.

Automation is destroying jobs and reshaping the economy; the cities are becoming centers of chaos; our resources continue to be allocated on the basis of profit rather than need; minorities are victimized by the economy and by society as well as by racist laws. These are only some of the most obvious of America's domestic crises. There are many others—in education, in civil liberties, in health costs, in the growth of bureaucracy in every area of our life—and these will be treated later in this platform. But there is one proposition basic to all our specific suggestions. That is our affirmation of the desperate need for democratic social planning.

Piecemeal reform loses much of its force by the very fact of its isolated character. Place a magnificent school in the midst of a slum—and leave untouched the educational impact of bad housing, low income, cultural deprivation and the like—and little will be accomplished. The crises facing America are so interrelated, so sweeping and comprehensive, that the only hope of progress lies in the creation of coherent, integrated programs.

Social Planning

We therefore propose that the United States of America adopt a policy of democratic social planning.

Specifically, we advocate the creation of comprehensive planning authorities in the critical areas of our life. In some cases this can be done within the framework of an existing agency—the Department of Health, Education, and Welfare, for instance. In others, it will require new institutions like the proposed Department of Urban Affairs. But whatever the locus of this planning, the important point is that it must be comprehensive and integrated.

We are not, however, simply for "planning." That can be done in the name of totalitarian dictatorship, or as a means of providing corporations with bigger profits. We are for planning with democratic social goals.

The adoption of a policy of democratic social planning must be based on a series of basic commitments:

• Planning for utilization of the resources of society to maintain full employment, and to allocate production for the satisfaction of human need;

• Planning with maximum opportunity for voluntary and local organizations to participate in decision making;

• Planning subject at all times to democratic control, i.e., subject to changes in the policies and personnel of planning authorities as determined by the people;

• Planning with a special charge to eradicate poverty in the

United States and particularly the poverty of racial and ethnic minorities.

The critics of democratic social planning see it as embodying the threat of a monstrous, bureaucratic state. We find this view naive. Bureaucracy is growing today in government, in the corporations, in the military, precisely because of lack of planning, because bureaucrats are not subject to popular control.

We see planning as a protection for individuals, as a way of decentralizing power. When the basic decisions of production and resource allocation become a matter of democratic political determination, that is not giving away power to some distant state. It is asserting the power of the people, of working men and women, over the huge, impersonal bureaucracies which now plan their lives.

We believe in the kind of planning that requires the complete democratization of the economy itself. So long as minority elites with enormous corporate power can "plan" for private profit and against the public interest, the democratic planning mechanism is extremely limited. In the long run, the great concentrations of economic power must be made public. However, we recognize that there is not sufficient sentiment for such a radical departure today. We therefore make our proposal for democratic social planning within the framework of those liberal and reform values espoused by the unions, the civil rights movement, the liberal movement, progressive farmers and important segments of religious opinion.

Finally we call attention to a number of glaring inequities, the remedying of which is a first urgency under democratic planning, and which certainly should be included among the unplanned piecemeal reforms now being urged. We join with trade unionists and liberals in demanding immediate action—

- For a higher minimum wage, from which farm labor must not be excluded;
- For an integrated national campaign against poverty, with

massive Federal aid to housing, community services, and education;

• For a program of public investment as an anti-recession measure;

• For an Area Redevelopment Bill to provide aid for distressed sections of the nation—a Point Four for our own underdeveloped regions;

• For a national resources policy which will extend the program which proved itself in the Tennessee Valley Authority to other areas of the country, such as the Columbia River Valley and the Missouri River Valley.

• For socialization of the oil industry on terms that give due regard to the needs and interests of a world peculiarly dependent upon oil. Today this industry is a power unto itself influencing domestic and foreign policy. Socialization of the oil industry must include social ownership of the oil fields.

• For socialization of basic means of transportation. We deplore and oppose the tendency to subsidize railroad passenger traffic while allowing private operators to reap the profits from freight traffic.

In making these demands, we note that the one piece of important social legislation passed since World War II, the Employment Act of 1946, is hardly more than a general statement of good intentions. In the post-war recessions, that Act failed to commit the Executive to any specific action, and the battle for meaningful remedies had to be fought anew each time in Congress. Therefore, we stand for a new law which will automatically require Executive action whenever unemployment rises: Federal spending for worthwhile social purposes, progressive tax relief for the broad mass of consumers, a government banking and finance policy to stimulate maximum investment, and so on.

PUBLIC FINANCE

Sources of Funds

Many Americans are appalled when they read proposals for vast new social programs. These, they argue, can only be paid for through an increase in income and excise taxes which will strike at the ordinary citizen.

We Socialists believe that this assumption is a sign of the low level of social and political creativity of our nation. A society with the technology and resources of the United States has ample production to finance a program of internal and international social development. The problem is to tap the real sources of wealth, not simply to tax the working men and women of America.

In two cases, we can specifically name enormous reservoirs of funds:

1. Success in a program of disarmament and disengagement would release billions for domestic and international social construction;

2. The planned allocation of resources, through the elimination of waste, would utilize existing capacity, both industrial and agricultural, to the full (it has been estimated that the last recession alone cost thirty-five billion dollars in terms of existing industrial capacity which was not put to use).

Yet, it can be argued that these two sources of funds wait upon considerable political changes, that they do not address themselves to urgent problems of finance for immediate programs. Even here, however, there are resources aplenty if only we had the vision to use them:

• Overhauling of the income tax laws with the view to making the income tax truly progressive, and the stopping-up of loop-holes designed to aid the rich;

• Progressive taxation of land increment resulting from social development rather than private improvement;

• Overhauling of land tax laws on the state level;

• Progressive taxation of undistributed corporate income;

- Strict accounting and reduction of corporate expense accounts, and on services given to executives as part of company policy;
- Ending favoritism to the oil industry, through legislation implementing the Supreme Court decision that off-shore oil is the property of the Federal government, and through termination of the special oil depletion allowance.

SOCIAL OWNERSHIP

These proposals, we must emphasize, are minimal and stopgap. The real problem is to make the enormous technology of the United States responsive to the needs of the whole people. Not only would the financing of social progress be greatly simplified by social ownership of major areas of the economy, but such socialization, when combined with economic decentralization, democratic control, and social planning for the needs of the people rather than the profits of a few, would go far toward giving our political democracy a sounder economic basis.

How much sounder for us to socialize steel, for example, than to use artificial and essentially undemocratic administrative pressure in a futile attempt to impose a sense of public responsibility on the major steel companies.

However essential such socialization of the major means of production is, there is an even more obvious and immediate need to bring under public ownership and democratic control the natural resources of our nation, such as gas and oil, and those natural monopolies such as railways and public utilities, and finally, the central banking system. We particularly express our vigorous opposition to the Kennedy plan for turning the communications satellite system over to private ownership, after it had been completely developed at public expense. We favor public ownership of the entire public communications system, including telephone and telegraph.

Socialists stress that social ownership of the major means of production is not a panacea for all our problems. There are great potential dangers in centralizing economic power. For this reason socialists lay particular stress on the decentralization of economic power where possible, and at all points a high degree of democratic control and social planning beginning at the community and place-of-work level.

The American labor movement faces a most critical period in the years ahead.

The jobs destroyed by automation tend to be in areas organized by the labor movement: these are the semi-skilled blue collar occupations which form the mass base of industrial unionism. As a result, the membership of the unions has stabilized or even declined, and the percentage of the work force which is organized has been waning for some time.

The unemployment caused by automation has a specific and new character: it is permanent. The labor movement is not confronted with a cyclical turn down, it cannot expect these displaced workers to return to the ranks of the unions under better circumstances. Their occupations have been abolished, and if the worker is forty years old or more, he has effectively been declared obsolete in our industrial society.

Given this enormous challenge, the traditional machinery of collective bargaining offers no hope for a real solution. The union's bargaining strength often declines along with the destruction of jobs and the loss of membership; the dislocations are of such a magnitude that, even if the economic power of the union were still as great as ever, remedies cannot be found on a company or industry level.

Labor Political Offensive

We believe that only a dynamic political offensive on the part of American labor can offer hope to the long term unemployed and to workers presently threatened by automation. The problems faced by the unions are national in scope and require democratic social planning if they are to be solved. In this context, labor can no longer regard political action as merely a means of maneuvering for this or that immediate advantage. It must come forth as the proponent of new departures, it must recapture the élan and vitality of the thirties in the process of creating a vast new popular movement for social change. This proposal, we believe, is not a "radical" one; it is imperative if the labor movement is to face the immediate, day to day challenge of automation.

In addition to a renewed commitment to political action, the labor movement must reject the proposals of labor-management "cooperation" now being put forth by the Administration. These ideas do not offer any real solution to the problems of the day, and in many cases, they are advanced at the expense of the poorest workers and the unemployed.

The proposal that labor and management must keep their negotiations within the limits of productivity gains has the effect of freezing the shares of the two contenders and thus canceling out the possibility of qualitative advance on the part of the workers. It also widens the gap between the employed, who get some share in the fruits of automation, and the unemployed who are essentially disregarded by this formula. In effect, the Administration has come up with a policy of compulsory arbitration (the compulsion is not legislative but informal, yet it is real) operating within narrow limits and solely oriented toward economic stability without any real consideration for social justice.

In this regard, we support the labor movement in its rejection of Administration policy and its advocacy of a thirty-five hour week. This approach cannot provide a basic solution to the problem of automation and unemployment, but it is an important immediate amelioration.

We also believe that the recent successes in the field of teacher unionism are extremely important. Given the changing character of the work force, these events have demonstrated the relevance of unionism to professional and white collar occupations. We believe that the labor movement must give much more support to these efforts than in the past.

The renewed use of court injunctions against strikes is more evidence of the need for political action, in this case against laws that throttle organizing efforts. Especially essential is repeal of laws forbidding strikes by underpaid teachers and hospital workers.

The problem of internal democracy within the labor movement continues to be a crucial one. The denial of opposition rights within some unions ends to deprive the labor movement of a major source of creativity and change.

We believe that the United Automobile Workers have indicated an important technique of promoting and defending union democracy: the Public Review Board. We feel that the entire labor movement should adopt this principle as part of a serious, continuing commitment to democracy and civil liberties in trade unions.

We support the right of staff members in the labor movement to organize unions of their own choosing.

We reject reactionary legislation, like the Landrum-Griffin Act, which utilizes the existence of admitted abuses within the unions in order to put over laws aimed against the labor movement as a whole. At the same time, we believe that there is a function for progressive legislation oriented at providing protection for the democratic rights of workers. Specifically, we believe that a "reserved powers" approach might well be a fruitful one: the law would describe a basic bill of internal union rights; unions which voluntarily met these standards through the adoption of institutions like the Public Review Board would be exempted from any intervention; the procedures would only be applied to those unions which refused to provide democratic guarantees on their own.

Finally, we continue to regard the labor movement as the greatest single potential source for social justice in American society. In the struggle between the unions and management, we are proudly partisan, taking the side of unionism. Whatever criticisms we make we are motivated by a desire to forward the labor movement, to help it live up to its own high promise.

AGRICULTURE

Some figures speak eloquently of the achievements and failures of American agriculture. In 1910 a farm worker produced enough food and fiber for 7 persons. By 1960 despite substantial increases in per capita consumption he produced enough to meet the needs of 24 persons. Between 1950 and 1960 farm output per man-hour rose 85 per cent. Such were the achievements of the effective use of machinery and scientific agriculture.

This great success has brought problems in its train. There is the problem, not truly of overproduction, but rather of poor distribution of goods and income in a hungry world. There is the problem of individual farmers who in large numbers have not been able to afford modern machinery. They have been felled by corporate farms.

Between 1950 and 1959 the number of farms in the United States dropped from 5.4 million to 3.7 million. According to a government report only about 25 per cent of the remaining family farms have the resources and productive capacity to return to their operators annual profits of $2,500. While family-owned and operated farms still constitute a numerical majority, 5 per cent of the nation's farms account for about 60 per cent of all vegetables produced for sale, nearly 50 per cent of the land in orchards and vineyards, and nearly 40 per cent of the total cotton crop. And this same 5 per cent pays over 70 per cent of the total farm wage bill.

Many of the great farms are owned like corporations by absentee owners. Many of them are "vertically integrated"; that is, a single company controls the entire chain between farmer and consumer. It is to these great farmers that the bulk of taxpayers' subsidies go under a system that made possible the exploits of Billie Sol Estes.

Various government agencies, for example the Rural Areas Development Board, the Areas Redevelopment Administration, the Farmers Home Administration, the Rural Electrification Administration, have programs to raise rural standards of

living and help small farmers. They are admittedly directed to
helping "the more fortunate of the disadvantaged." Most of
them depend on local initiative, which in effect means the
approval of the local power structure of a given rural area;
that is, of the more prosperous farmers, in the South always
white. As of June 1962, less than 100 under-employed farm
workers have received training under A.R.A. for available jobs
operating and maintaining farm machinery. Extension of the
program has been blocked by local power elites.

The problem of the small farmers driven off their land despite the billions paid to subsidize agriculture by no means
stands alone. There is the special problem of the low economic
conditions of sharecroppers, and what has become in recent
years the larger problem of hired farm labor, much of it de-
prived of minimum wage protection, and in varying degrees
of some other protections afforded other workers.

In the face of the complicated problems of agriculture we
renew our socialist insistence that the basis of land ownership
should be occupancy and use; that cooperative farming should
be encouraged as against corporation farming; the family-type
farms where conditions are favorable should be more effectively aided under existing agencies with a great increase of
activities under the Farmers Home Administration. We call
for the full enforcement of the 160 acre limitation of the Recla-
mation Act restricting water from federally financed reclama-
tion projects to family-size farms.

We oppose programs which seek to foster scarcity in a hungry world as a means of higher incomes to farmers.

Within the U.S. we seek enlargement of school lunch programs and other public welfare food programs in rural areas
as well as cities.

Internationally our food "surpluses" should be used to fight
hunger. As far as possible such a program should be adminis-
tered through the U.N. to assure that food will be a weapon in
a war against human misery, not in the cold war.

Farm Labor

We demand for hired labor on farms minimum wage legislation and other protective laws at least equivalent to those in force for industrial workers. Minimum wage legislation would help, not hurt, family farmers most of whom in contrast to the "factories in the fields" employ little or no such labor. In the Mississippi delta on small-scale farms the cost of hired labor is about 10 per cent of total operating costs against 30 per cent on the large plantations. We urge prompt passage of the ten bills introduced in the U.S. Senate to give at least a modest protection to farm laborers. More is necessary.

We call for an end to the program under which hundreds of thousands of foreign contract farm workers are imported annually. There is no need for these workers and their employment serves to depress wages and conditions and to deprive domestic workers of needed employment. Foreign workers have at times been used illegally to break a number of strikes in fields and packing sheds. These imported workers are not free agents and are themselves badly exploited. Most of them come from Mexico under Public Law 78. This law expires at the end of 1963 and should under no circumstances be renewed.

Congress should enact a program to facilitate recruitment of domestic migratory workers under guarantees of minimum wages, etc., better than those provided for Mexican workers, which at present give to these imported workers somewhat better guarantees than many domestic workers have found. Contrary to the claims of the 2 per cent of the nation's farmers who import farm workers, Public Law 78 has produced only incidental benefits for Mexican farm workers and the Mexican economy. The government is obliged to do what it can under the Alliance for Progress and various U.N. programs to help to improve the general condition of the Mexican workers.

We heartily commend the organizing campaign of the AFL-CIO among farm workers but urge that it be extended and given even greater priority.

HEALTH, EDUCATION AND WELFARE

Medical Care

Medical needs are so essential, and their costs are so capricious and unpredictable, that we should long since have provided for them socialistically in the same matter-of-fact way that we socialistically protect ourselves against crime and fire. And in this opinion above all others, we Socialists are confident we speak for the great bulk of the American people, who throughout this century have consistently favored every medical reform that was offered. The absence of socialized medicine in this country is disgraceful evidence of the power of a moneyed minority to thwart democratic processes.

The permanent crisis in medical costs reflects basic changes in technology and the economy, and cannot be confronted in any basic sense by piecemeal legislation. Current reform proposals are too little and too late, and sometimes wrongheaded. Especially alarming is the effort to use tax funds to swell the coffers of private insurance companies.

Present proposals for Social Security health benefits are good as far as they go, but do not go far enough even within the framework of their own limitations. At very least they should include medical, surgical, dental, and psychiatric fees. Funeral expenses should be assisted. And we are distressed that hospitalization payments should be limited as to time: Those who need more than 90 days of hospital care are few and represent very little money in national terms, but the private tragedy is immense. For humanitarian reasons we support the current proposals as the best of a bad lot, and we welcome the precedent of paying for health costs through Social Security mechanisms; but we insist that at best it is only an inadequate stopgap.

What we need—what even less prosperous nations have long enjoyed—is insurance through tax funds for the best possible medical care for every man, woman, and child. We call upon Americans everywhere to work with us for this goal.

We urge a system of socialized medicine under which the citizen is free to choose the doctor and the type of care he desires. We would encourage, through tax incentives and other measures, cooperative and other plans under which physicians are hired on a salary basis to provide complete medical care; a total divorcement of payments from medical procedures is essential if we are to achieve in fact the ideal of preventive care which science has now made possible. Yet fee-for-service piecework medicine should be allowed to continue where the people in a given community want it. For administration of socialized medicine should be local, with the public participating democratically, and the Federal government should confine itself to providing funds and regulating standards.

We favor drastic government action in support of the costs of medical education. The ranks of the medical profession must no longer be restricted to those who are born into well-to-do families. We favor subsidy of the costs of training nurses and medical technologists. We favor a decent wage scale for hospital workers, and defend their right to form unions and to strike: It is scandalous that hospitals should subsidize themselves by sweating their employees. We support, and favor extension of, present government hospital-building programs; every community should possess a medical center with emergency-ward and nursing-home facilities.

Prescribed drugs must be available to all citizens without cost to them. An independent government corporation should enter and become a major competitive entity in the pharmaceutical industry. At the same time, drug companies should continue to receive financial incentives for genuine pharmaceutical research. The government should engage much more heavily in pharmaceutical research. It must be far more stringent in its licensing of drugs.

Education

A democratic society requires an educational system which gives to each child opportunity for maximum development of all his potentialities. If we want a free and democratic society, our education must be free and democratic in principle, in classroom practice, and in school administration.

Remarkable technical progress has been achieved by scientists, technicians, production managers and workers. They are the products of our present-day schools. Our schools have not done badly in promoting and increasing the intellectual and technical knowledge of the human race. What has broken down is the capacity of knowing what to do with this knowledge.

What we need is education which will inspire youth with values of interhuman relations, with social interests, with respect for the worth and the dignity of each and every human being, with confidence in man's ability to solve his problems cooperatively with his fellowman.

We reject the demand, made popular by Russia's launching of the Sputniks, for gearing our educational system to the needs of a war machine, or for imitating the narrow objectives of education in the Soviet Union and other totalitarian states. We believe in education for the whole man, education geared to the aptitude of each student and designed to produce well-informed citizens capable of thinking for themselves and participating responsibly in the rights and duties of citizenship.

We reject the idea that equal educational opportunities, the promoting of creativity, cooperation, mutual aid, and welfare are the "grave diggers of education"; we believe rather that equal and not separated opportunities for every child are not only essential for democratic education, but also promote best the selection and education of the gifted on the broadest possible foundation. We oppose all attempts to break up our universal democratic education, whether by so-called equal but separate schools, or by underhand pedagogical assumptions that different environmental and class mentalities require the splitting of schools into those for middle- and upper-class children and those for low-income or slum children.

We favor Federal aid for school construction, for higher

teacher salaries, and for guidance services in public education.
We favor a Federal college scholarship plan on the basis of
ability only. We oppose giving Federal aid to communities
which refuse to integrate their school system as required by
the May, 1954 decision of the Supreme Court. We favor the
extension of unionism among teachers. We oppose loyalty
oaths in schools and colleges, for either teachers or students,
because their only effect is to create a climate of suspicion
incongruous to education in a free society. We also strongly
condemn R.O.T.C. as military conditioning wholly inappro-
priate to education in a democracy. We urge expansion of
experimental remedial and guidance programs supported by
local, state, and federal funds, and governmental support of
more adequate training for teachers.

Welfare

Our society is the first in history possessing the power to
obliterate poverty in its entirety. Yet one-third of us are poor,
one-fifth of us dwell in uttermost poverty, and the rest of us
are too busy boasting of affluence to see them. Thus ours is
also the first society in history to forget that the poor exist.

We ignore the needs of growing millions of urban and rural
workers made obsolete by automation, rejected by the very
processes that enrich the rest of us. We adopt pitiful halfway
measures for the millions of old people made wretched by
loneliness, dependency, and constant fear of medical catastrophe. The terrible poverty of minority groups we accept as
part of the American tradition. We first create the poor, then
we keep them poor, and then we blame them for their poverty.

What is required of us is a concerted attack on poverty in
all its forms, and adoption of two principles: A decent minimum standard for all, and maximum protection against economic mischance. What the poor too often get, when they are
not ignored, are heartless pinch-penny policies, and welfare
approaches which demean them, until we have produced a
whole class of Americans who have come to expect to be
pushed around.

In the area of public assistance our most pressing need is to abolish forthwith, in those states where they still survive, those barbaric laws or administrative regulations which—

Allow relief files to be inspected by the general public;

Require the publication of names of relief recipients;

Deny assistance on grounds of "employability" where no effort is made to find jobs for the unemployed as part of the assistance process;

Deny assistance to unwed mothers or illegitimate children;

Impose requirements as to length of residence;

Require the sale by relief applicants of the tools of their trade;

Deny assistance because applicants possess property which cannot be quickly converted into cash;

Require contributions from relatives other than parents of minor children;

Use current rent as a "means test" for eligibility in localities where there is a shortage of low-cost housing.

In those public-assistance programs in which the Federal government participates (old-age assistance, aid to dependent children, and aid to the blind and disabled) we demand amendment of the Social Security Act to withhold funds from states permitting the above practices.

We call for amendment of the Social Security Act to provide for Federal participation in programs of general (noncategorical) assistance.

These are minimal demands made in the name of common decency. But if we are to conduct a war against the poverty in our midst, our welfare laws must go much further as part of a broad-scale multi-front program.

Unemployment

Unemployment compensation must be made available to all citizens who cannot find work, for as long as they remain jobless. Payments must be high enough to support a minimum

decent standard of living, and all payments must be pegged
to the cost-of-living index. It is the duty of society, through
its agencies of government, to provide socially useful work
for all who are willing and able to work. This problem should
be approached from the standpoint of the needs and aspirations of *each individual* unemployed person.

Social Security

Social Security (O.A.S.I.) should not be, as it is today,
merely a palliative measure designed to supplement the savings and pensions (often nonexistent) of retired citizens. It
must become a true national pension plan, supplying the full
economic security necessary for a dignified and fruitful old
age, and available to all regardless of prior contributions in
taxes. Allowances must not be reducible on account of additional earned income. Maternal and child services must be
greatly expanded. Orphan beneficiaries, for whom payments
now lapse when they reach age 18, must have access to a
special fund for educational scholarships or for training for
a trade, and benefits must continue on behalf of those engaged
in such training until age 21. Social Security taxation must
apply to every dollar of income and must be graduated to rest
more heavily upon higher incomes. All payments must be
pegged to the cost-of-living index.

Other Problems

• Tobacco advertising and labelling must be brought under
stringent government controls, must specify tar and nicotine
content, and must include notice of medical hazard.
• Narcotics addiction and alcoholism must be treated as
sicknesses, not crime. Federal government must initiate special
health programs for narcotics addicts, tied to job training and
placement services. More basically, we urge adoption of the
system used in some other countries of permitting addicts to
register as such and buy their drugs at regulated prices in
government addiction control centers; our present laws succeed only in nurturing the criminal underworld, forcing se-

cretiveness upon addicts, and ultimately in spreading addiction.

• Our society teaches concepts of economic selfishness and ruthless competition which promote many expressions of crime. It creates an underworld of poverty, from within which, criminality appears to offer the only real hope of escape. Society shall not be permitted to hide from itself its own responsibility for much of the crime in our midst. The legitimate protection of society against its deviates and criminals is one thing; quite something else is the attitude of smug righteousness behind which so many Americans neglect man's eternal responsibility for other men in trouble.

Crime prevention begins in eradicating the societal and environmental causes of criminal behavior. We must eliminate all the various patterns of preferential treatment for wealthy offenders as against poor ones, as regards bail, legal council, fines, etc. We urge the institution of a full-scale program for rehabilitation of criminals. We are opposed to the punitive rather than the rehabilitative approach to criminal jurisprudence, and consequently we regard capital punishment as a grim and uncivilized vestige of the past. We pledge ourselves to work for its eradication.

• Legal council must be free for all who need it. Bail and fines must be adjusted to the financial resources of the offender. Our laws in practice work prejudicially against the poor, the underprivileged, members of minority groups, the uneducated, the ill-favored. A deliberate effort to counter this prejudice is an important goal of Socialism.

• It cannot be expected that our competitive and segregated society will effectively prevent juvenile delinquency. However, we urge the immediate provision of ample Federal financial aid for carefully prepared projects for preventing and treating juvenile delinquency.

CIVIL LIBERTIES

As Socialists, we stand for democracy in every aspect of life; the democratization of the economy and the society as well as of politics. Therefore the defense of civil liberties is basic to our philosophy.

In addition, we are confident that Communism, like other anti-democratic ideas and movements, can be met and defeated in free ideological and political struggle. "Anti-Communist" legislation and marathon legislative investigations of "subversive propaganda" strike at basic rights of free speech, press and political association. They deprive us of our democratic creativity, and thus weaken us in the struggle against totalitarianism.

Given these principles, we urge: repeal of the Smith Act and pardon for all of its victims; repeal of the McCarran "Communist control" act; abolition of the Attorney General's "subversive" list; repeal of loyalty oaths for students and faculty members; abolition of the House Committee on Un-American Activities and the Senate Internal Security Committee.

CIVIL RIGHTS

Civil rights remains the foremost domestic issue of our time. If anything fresh and promising has appeared on the American scene since the mid-fifties, it has been the pressing upsurge of American Negroes demanding rights that are constitutionally theirs. We support wholeheartedly this movement and reject categorically the notion that these rights can be in any way compromised in the name of progress on other fronts.

In the past two years the dramatic sit-in movement has not diminished but has entered a new phase. It has expanded from lunch counters to theaters, to libraries, to companies that discriminate, and finally to voter registration. Spearheaded by the Congress of Racial Equality (C.O.R.E.) and the Student Nonviolent Coordinating Committee (S.N.C.C.), direct action has continued while political action has begun. It is not now just statutory Jim Crow that is being challenged. The whole rotten structure of white supremacy with its one-party system is being shattered. Today in the South there are boycotts going on (against job discrimination, as well as segregated travel) that are more broadly based than the original Montgomery protest: in Albany and Macon, Georgia; Jackson, Mississippi; and Birmingham, Alabama.

In all of this, the Administration has played a double role. On the one hand it can rightly point to accomplishments (some Department of Justice suits; federal protection for the freedom riders in Montgomery; the President's Commission on Employment) which go beyond anything of the Eisenhower years. But on the other hand, the Administration has failed, and failed miserably, in really responding to the profound challenge of civil rights.

The Department of Justice suits on voter registration have been limited in number, concentrated in areas where there is a white majority (and avoiding the crucial battles in the black majority areas where S.N.C.C. has been working primarily), and on an individual case-by-case basis. In almost two years the President has refused the "stroke of the pen," which he spoke of during the campaign: federal funds still go for the support of housing, as well as school, segregation. It is typical of the administration to be suing for voting booth integration in Georgia, while appointing racist judges in Louisiana and Mississippi.

In Congress, the administration has refused to redeem the pledges of the 1960 Democratic Party platform. While young people have given a magnificent demonstration of courage and creativity, the White House and Capitol Hill have been engaged in business as usual.

Nonviolent Action

We are proud that Socialists have supported the work of the Congress of Racial Equality, the National Association for the Advancement of Colored People, the Southern Christian Leadership Conference and the Student Nonviolent Coordinating Committee.

Out of the action-oriented climate generated by the spontaneous sit-ins have sprung the Freedom Rides, initiated by C.O.R.E. and joined by S.N.C.C. and the Southern Christian

Leadership Conference. We congratulate C.O.R.E. and the
other groups who organized the freedom rides, and we salute
the heroic freedom riders themselves. While we give all-out
support to the freedom rides (whether along Route 40 or to
McComb, Mississippi) we simultaneously recognize that in
the last analysis their success will be determined by the extent to which they stimulate activity on the part of the masses
of Negroes who live in the South. Along with S.N.C.C. and
C.O.R.E. our aim must be to always broaden the base of the
movement and to stimulate mass action. The vast potential of
the movement will not be fulfilled until the great mass of
unorganized working-class Negroes are actively mobilized.

The emergence of the Negro American Labor Council is
another extremely important and positive development. Negroes in the United States are the victims of a double discrimination: through Jim Crow statutes and through a racist
economy which has imprisoned the minorities in the dirtiest,
most unstable and low-paying jobs. The N.A.L.C. reflects both
of these determinants of Negro life. It is dedicated to trade
unionism, to a really integrated trade-union movement; and
it demands that labor live up to its own ideals, that Jim Crow
within the unions be struck down and a campaign waged to
open up skilled jobs to Negroes and other minority groups.
We concur heartily in this program.

Black Nationalism

There is a rising tide of black nationalism in the Negro
community today. The nationalists are not only recruiting and
organizing at a faster rate than other organizations, they are
reaching people unreached by traditional protest organizations
—workers, the unemployed and young people. We reject the
idea of a black nation and racism of any variety. We oppose
the separation of the races as incompatible with the socialist
ideal. Yet, we recognize that nationalism grows where liberalism is strongest, where the promise has been made and broken,
where the laws are integrationist and education, housing and
employment are segregated. Responsibility for the growth of

the nationalist and Muslim groups also rests in part with the integrationist organizations. Their inability to make contact with and mobilize the mass of unorganized and frustrated working-class Negroes who are crowded into the slums of our cities has created the vacuum which the Muslims are trying to fill. The solution is not persecution of the Muslims but an all-out assault on segregation and employment discrimination, a movement based on bread and butter issues in the North as well as the South. At present only the N.A.L.C. appears to be cognizant of the need for developing a mass-action program aimed at these problems. The cry of the nationalists for violence has only reaffirmed our belief in tactical non-violence. The result of their attitude has been a withdrawal from the real fight, which is the fight of all decent Americans for complete integration and democracy.

The fact that the Southern students have turned to politics in their voter registration drive has given impetus to Negro candidacies in the South. We support these representatives of the civil rights movement in their challenge to the lily-white one-partyism below the Mason Dixon line. We believe that their success is of vital importance to American political life in general, for it opens up the possibility of smashing the Dixiecrat-Republican alliance, of shattering the bastion of reaction which has developed in the American South.

With all of this progress, the great fact remains that American politics have not been equal to this greatest moral imperative of our national life. Both parties have reneged on their campaign promises of 1960. We pledge ourselves to put human rights first and to work for the immediate passage of legislation which would:

• Guarantee the right to vote with the power of action vested, once a pattern of discrimination is found, in the Executive;

• Commit the Federal Government to initiate legal action on behalf of school integration, voting rights or any other civil right;

- Deny Federal funds to any segregated institution or program;
- Implement Section 2 of the Fourteenth Amendment, depriving states of representation in proportion to the number of citizens they deprive of the right to vote on account of race, color, or previous servitude.

In addition to these immediate civil rights proposals, we realize that the goal of human equality cannot be attained in an ill-housed, ghetto-ized society with inferior education for the minorities. We therefore urge that Federal programs for low-cost housing and aid to education contain provisions specifically directed toward making these social solutions a means of integration. We support those Negroes in the North who are challenging the mockery and hypocrisy of de facto segregation in the midst of rhetorical avowals of civil rights.

Finally, we Socialists pledge, not only our political thinking and action, but our personal participation in this magnificent movement for freedom.

Other Minorities

Mexican-Americans, Puerto Ricans, and other minority groups are also the victims of discrimination. We support the democratic movement of all these minorities as part of the united struggle for the principle of equality for all.

We are opposed to the current effort to deprive American Indians of their remaining community lands and resources. Premature and enforced assimilation of Indians into the dominant culture is no answer to their special problems. No major programs affecting Indians should be launched without the free consent of the tribes or bands involved. As a first step to alleviate sufferings and amend ancient wrongs, we endorse the proposal of the National Congress of American Indians, for a "Point Four" program for Indians.

Ballot Access

We advocate a Constitutional amendment guaranteeing the right of ready ballot access in all states to minority political parties.

Conscription

Hostility to peacetime conscription in the Old World was one of the great forces motivating immigration to this country, and Americans have traditionally regarded it as alien and a threat to freedom. Under the conditions of modern military technology it cannot even be justified on grounds of need. It serves only to maintain the power of military bureaucracy and to subject a portion of the populace each year to military conditioning. We demand its immediate abolition.

URBAN PROBLEMS

Migration from the farms to the cities is accelerating as technological change continues to make small farms more and more unprofitable. To this has been joined further migrations caused by industrial change and regional unemployment. Concurrently, middle-income people are continuing to flee from the cities. Thus increasingly America's poor are being concentrated in urban centers.

This has aggravated problems which already were not being met, or were being met improperly. Our cities are largely unpleasant places to live, and here as elsewhere the fault lies in the lack of adequate social planning.

Thus, pressure from business and real estate interests has led to an emphasis on facilities for motor transport. Highway construction has been given priority over community needs while there has been little if any concern with the problems of mass transportation. Existing mass low-cost transportation facilities have been allowed to deteriorate. It is, as always, the poor who are victimized by this process.

Thus, the national policies of public housing and urban renewal and redevelopment have lost their original purpose of eliminating slums and providing housing for low-income fami-

266 Socialism Re-examined

lies. Government programs are now used by real estate promoters, mortgage and banking interests, builders and contractors for their own private profit. These interests have virtually stopped low-income public housing in all but the largest Northern cities; in the South these public programs are used to further segregation of Negroes. The primary purpose of urban renewal and development now is to have the public purse buy and assemble lands to sell cheap to redevelopment corporations for costly apartment houses or for commercial developments which will "enrich the city's tax base." Those displaced by this process are, as always, the poor, whose societal relations are disrupted, who are forced from one slum to another.

Thus, there has been a massive failure in enforcing health, housing, building, and fire codes, because old-party politicians do not want to interfere with the enormous profits of slum landlords, because they will not raise enough taxes to pay for health and sanitation, because inspectors are selected for political loyalties rather than for competence. It is the poor, the underpaid, the underprivileged whose very lives, and the futures of whose children, are endangered.

Thus cities continue to rely upon sales taxes and other backward-looking methods of raising funds, whose common denominator is that they hit the poorest hardest.

The accepted theory in America today is that cities exist solely as a place for someone to make money or earn his keep. All other interests are considered secondary.

We Socialists regard cities as a place where human life can have a new and better meaning in a world at peace. They are the arena in which humanity can finally meet and destroy the ancient enemies of disease, want, ignorance, squalor, and ugliness.

We propose a program of rebuilding the cities of America to meet the human needs of the people who live in them.

A Program for the City

As steps to meet the problems of urban growth and change we advocate:

1. A new national policy of population distribution in which fewer people will be concentrated in the great metropolitan areas, and in which there will be a larger number of cities ranging in size from 25,000 to 100,000 in population. We propose the restoration of populations to areas which have lost population by giving incentives to industry to relocate in depressed areas, and by relocating governmental and other agencies in places outside of the great metropolitan areas. We propose to use the Area Redevelopment Agency to foster this objective.

2. Re-establishment of the National Resources Planning Board to properly coordinate the use of resources and their distribution from area to area.

3. Creation by the Federal government of regional planning agencies in cooperation with state and local governments, to supervise over-all planning for all Federal expenditures in public improvements. These agencies shall help each region to help itself and shall especially concern themselves with the problems of water resources, water and air pollution, land use and land pollution, orderly urban development, and convenient public transportation.

4. A Department of Urban Affairs with cabinet rank in the Federal government.

5. A Department of Urban Affairs in each state government.

6. Federal sponsorship of satellite cities to reduce urban congestion and to provide a decent environment for the rearing of children and the enjoyment of life.

7. Creation of regional metropolitan governments in the major metropolitan areas to coordinate the fragmented, inefficient, and competing governments in such areas.

8. Encouraging state governments to take a more active role in solving urban problems in the interests of the people rather than the special interests.

9. Implementation of the Supreme Court order for states to provide for better apportionment of legislative seats.

10. Federal matching funds for planning, sewage control, waterworks, expansion and mass transportation.

11. Public ownership and non-profit operation of power and transportation utilities.

12. A Federal master plan for removing in the next ten years all sub-standard housing, urban or rural. Sufficient federal, state, and local government appropriations to make this plan feasible. Public participation in the formation of the master plan and local interpretation of it.

13. An adequate program of public housing, with better architecture and less density of land use, integrated as to neighborhoods; without segregation as to race or income level; with some of the housing located on new lands in order to reduce costs.

14. More concern for persons displaced by public works or renewal projects, as to the right of better housing, and as to protection from the brutal disruption of their lives in established neighborhoods. More concern for small businesses and enterprises forced to relocate by public works projects. Special procedures, required by law, to guard their interests.

15. Application of the principle that the rental value of land is a social creation and should be appropriated by taxation for social purposes. All housing projects should insure a continuous return to the local government of increases in values created by public investment.

16. Sanctions against the creation of income or racial ghettoes. Grants-in-aid should be withheld where discrimination of any kind exists.

17. Approaches that will foster the idea of community, and encourage democratic participation of citizens in community decisions.

18. Encouragement of Rochdale cooperative housing under user sponsorship, eliminating the private entrepreneurs who are constructing cooperative multiple dwellings for the construction profits.

19. Aid for lower and middle income home-owners who are able to refurbish existing homes as part of the program of community renewal.

20. Special programs for the housing of the aged, the economically displaced and the socially backward.

21. Federal grants-in-aid to universities and colleges and scientific institutes to engage in continuous and fundamental research on the problems of urbanization and the meaning of urbanization.

LEISURE AND COMMUNICATIONS

The technological revolution of our times makes possible a society of increasing leisure. If our enormous resources were allocated democratically and on the basis of social planning, we could look forward to a rapid and progressive decrease in the number of working hours along with an increase in the standard of living.

And yet, this prospect comes as a threat to our society. In this area, as in almost every other, our social and political thinking lags far behind our technological genius. The leisure we produce seems to be empty, unhuman, sterile.

Leisure today is not a problem as any "natural" consequence of modern technology. Our leisure facilities, and above all our means of communication, are organized like everything else in this society, to enhance the profit of the few. Madison Avenue is not an evil conspiracy of mean men with bad taste. It is an inevitable institution in a society which prefers to manufacture and manipulate pseudo-need, which can be satisfied at a fat profit, to dealing with real and desperate needs.

Broadly then, we Socialists believe that leisure time must be taken away from the control of the corporate minorities; that we must socially allocate resources for free time; that improving the quality of life is one of the main aims of our movement.

Specifically today we propose:

• The formation of a Federal television network, nationally owned and dedicated to high standards of entertainment and public discussion which will provide competition to the private stations, with participation by the talent unions in the establishment of program policy;

• The integration of entertainment and leisure in urban planning; provisions for retaining existing and new community centers and neighborhood gathering places; the planning of parks and recreational facilities with Federal assistance; a national research program into imaginative techniques of community recreation for children and adults such as those found in Denmark and Norway;

• A National Theatre and Ballet; a subsidy program directed to helping actors and theatres who provide entertainment of a high aesthetic merit which is not now commercially profitable (the "Off-Broadway" theatre is an example of this kind of production);

• The preservation and social use of forests, beaches, etc., in a vastly expanded national conservation and park program.

FOREIGN POLICY

American foreign policy must be based upon two inescapable facts: (1) We live in a world so interdependent that men's struggle for freedom, justice, and the conquest of bitter poverty must be universal; and (2) In that struggle, thanks to our scientific progress in the art of destruction, nation states will use the time-honored method of war only at peril to the very life of our race.

Powers possessed of nuclear weapons will not fight without using them, and to use them means mutual destruction almost beyond the power of our imagination to contemplate. The days when one could face a realistic choice between peace and freedom or peace and justice, using the ancient institution of war as a cruel instrument, are gone. Men for brief periods may have peace, i.e., the absence of war, without freedom; they cannot in today's world have freedom without peace.

Thus, the necessities of the cold war push us in America further into the status of a garrison state at grave cost to a sane economy and to our civil liberties. It was none other than Dwight Eisenhower, General of the Army and Republican President who in his Farewell Message warned us solemnly against the military-industrial complex already so powerful. In a struggle against it we, the people, may win battles. We shall not win the final victory because the cold war, emotionally and practically, requires a military-industrial complex to serve it. Only the end of great wars, hot and cold, will make possible truly cooperative commonwealths or a world-wide federation of them.

In this modern world there can be no hard and fast line between foreign and domestic policy. A policy based on cold war gives us the garrison state. A domestic policy which gives the lie to our professions of democracy and equality of rights, and builds an economy which for all our boasted affluence leaves two-fifths of our people below the line of oppressive poverty, is crippled in its struggle against communist or fascist aggression throughout the world. It is in the light of these truths as well as of our great national wealth that our general trade as well as our cold-war policies should be examined.

The great communist drive for power, aided by some American blunders, is now the absorbing concern of the American government and people. But we Socialists repeat our insistence in our 1960 platform that if there were no communist imperialism to compete with what we miscall "free enterprise," that is, a far-flung capitalism, there would be great strains on peace because of the tremendous "revolution of rising expectations" which expresses itself most forcibly in revolt against colonialism but also against an intolerable burden of poverty and economic exploitation. It is one of the happier facts of the years since 1945 that so much imperialism has been liquidated with so little violence. For this mankind owes more than it realizes to the British government under the Labor Party.

The Colonial Yoke

There remain, however, important areas to be freed from the colonial yoke; and to those who struggle in them for freedom the Socialist Party pledges its sympathy and all forms of practicable support.

In the Congo we approve in general the present policy of the United Nations. An independent Congo should not be the creature either of international communism or of capitalist mining interests working behind native rulers.

In Algeria we applaud the settlement worked out by de Gaulle and the Moslem Algerian government. We condemn with horror the brutal terrorism practiced or encouraged by European Algerians and call upon America's ally, France, to use whatever strength is required to crush this despicable European resistance in order that the terms of settlement may be honorably carried out. We thank the Moslems in Algeria for their extraordinary restraint, under provocation deliberately intended to drive them into counter-violence and a renewal of war. (*Since this platform was adopted peace has been consummated between France and Algeria, but a constructive program for a weary people has been jeopardized by internal factional strife. Political independence is no social cure-all.*)

The immediate threat of a large-scale war of annihilation rises from communist aggression. That aggression is backed by enormous military power in Russia and China—two communist nations which, however, because of differences between them, are far from constituting completely unified power. Yet the great gains of communism since World War II have not resulted from Russian armed aggression (although Russian force was outrageously used against rebellion in Hungary), but by victories within nations in which strong parties have first been won to communist ideology. This type of aggression cannot successfully be fought by nuclear bombs.

Our great battle with communism is ideological and it cannot be won by identifying democracy and respect for human rights with capitalism—not even with the somewhat modified capitalism which prevails in America after the New Deal, and its establishment of a welfare state by the appropriation of ideas formerly regarded as socialist. American propaganda for democracy against the ruthless communist totalitarianism suffers enormously from the facts that 1) so many Americans debase democracy and freedom to the level of mere anti-communism, and include such nations as Saudi Arabia and Franco's Spain among the free people; 2) they persist in volubly (and falsely) equating democratic socialism and totalitarian communism; 3) so obviously many of communism's haters in this country act from love of power and private profit rather than from any true love of mankind.

Socialism Versus Communism

The Socialist Party renews its insistence that in democratic socialism lies the strongest defense against communist totalitarianism, cruelty, and disregard of human rights. To the degree that the U. S. by its policy shores up dictators, corrupt governments, and great landlords in the underdeveloped sections of the world it invites a defeat which no attainable military strength can indefinitely forestall. What the U. S. needs and what capitalism, decked out as "free enterprise," cannot supply is a philosophy of human development in underdeveloped lands.

Peace has been the subject of eloquent and doubtless subjectively sincere speeches by our President and other high officials. But actions speak louder than words. Our nation claims great superiority in nuclear weapons, but it has inaugurated fresh tests. It insists on its right to tamper with the universe by high "rainbow" explosions affecting the Van Allen radiation belt despite vigorous objections by British and other scientists. It drives forward on a shelter campaign, proclaiming its hope that 40 million of our citizens might emerge from man-made shelters into a horror of destruction.

All of this does far more to increase the danger of war than to guarantee any safety. Our policy in action seems to much of the world the posture of a nation ready to consider thermonuclear war, even pre-emptive war, if it does not have its way.

The lifeline to peace must be braided of four strong strands: 1) universal disarmament down to a police level for preserving peace in nations and between nations; 2) a steady strengthening of international organization, the United Nations, so that it can substitute law for war in our present anarchic world of absolute nation-states; 3) orderly disengagement from American military commitments around the world which are more likely to lead to war than peace; 4) increased engagement in the holy war against poverty, illiteracy and disease around the world.

Disarmament

In the popular mind all over the world disarmament is most intimately tied to peace. Support for it is growing, and with reason. The world is no safer, while nations play with nuclear, chemical, and bacteriological weapons, than a kindergarten where children play with loaded revolvers. Armament races may be originally the expression rather than the causes of national fears and suspicions, but often they in themselves have tended to be causes of war—so the British Foreign Secretary, Lord Grey, declared the Anglo-German naval race to be before World War I—and unquestionably total disarmament along the U. S.-Canadian border contributed mightily to settlement of bitter boundary disputes. Almost all the world has given lip service to disarmament. It has been subject to repeated unsuccessful negotiation since World War II. However, the Soviet Union and the U. S. have agreed to principles of disarmament and the Antarctic continent is subject to an effective treaty, barring military experimentation on it. The Soviet Union and the U. S. have at last placed their respective programs, worked out in considerable detail, before the Geneva conference of 1962.

Yet agreement at that conference is unlikely. The nations are too far apart on procedures and timing. And though there is great public acceptance of the desirability of disarmament and what Eisenhower, Khrushchev, and Kennedy have all called the "unthinkability" of war, as yet there is neither an emotional nor practical basis for effective general disarmament in the attitudes of governments or peoples; nor will they yet accept any substitute for the grim arbitrament of war in their conflicts.

On the contrary, there is in the U. S. another obstacle to disarmament and that is the ironic fact that on the arms race, which does so much to keep the world poor, so many Americans believe their jobs and their prosperity depend—this in a world in which, properly used, a relatively small proportion of the 117 billion dollars spent annually by nations rich and poor on their arms races might rapidly wipe out poverty.

It is essential to disarmament that there be in this country an economic program for the transition from the arms race to a peace race. The newly constituted Disarmament Agency should be instructed to keep such a program up-to-date.

If we must expect the final treaty on disarmament to drag there is the more reason to keep up pressure for continuing or renewing negotiations. Meanwhile the U. S. can do a great deal to change the climate of negotiation by what have been called unilateral initiatives, that is, acts toward peace not in themselves destroying our military might but clearly showing our desire to end the cold war on its military level. The greatest of these acts would have been if the U. S., the power which initiated atomic war, should have refused to add to its immense capacity to overkill by further tests in the atmosphere. These tests carried on by any nation on whatever excuse constitute a kind of declaration of war on mankind by reason of the dangers to the living and their descendants in further nuclear fallout. In thus answering the iniquitous Russian tests, our government assured further Soviet tests and opened wide the door to the nuclear club. Thereby it has made more likely the fulfillment of Sir Charles P. Snow's prediction that with the continuation of tests "in six years other nations, including China, will have the bombs and in ten some will go off."

The struggle against "tests, East or West" must go on and it should be supplemented by other acts of the United States to show how sincerely we seek to lessen tensions and make possible a general disarmament backed by the citizenry of the world. The Socialist Party pledges itself to a policy of thorough discussion of such initiatives and active support of realistic proposals.

Strengthening the U.N.

We do not think it possible or desirable at this juncture in history to set up a world government as centralized in power as the U. S. now is. We do think it possible, and essential, to strengthen the U. N. in the confidence of the peoples and in its power to substitute law for war. This is in part a matter of education of the people in our own and other countries. The U. N. was founded on the gamble that the Big Three, the U. S. A., the U. S. S. R., and the United Kingdom, which held together to win the war, would hold together to maintain the peace. This hope was frustrated by the rapidly developing cleavage responsible for the cold war, sharply accentuated by Stalin's tactics. The vital Security Council was rendered almost useless by repeated Soviet vetoes. The wonder is that the U. N. and its agencies have done as well as they have in serving peace and promoting international cooperation.

The U. S. can immediately strengthen the U. N. by its purchase of bonds as originally proposed by President Kennedy and by its repeal of the Connally reservations under which our government makes itself judge of what cases involving it, it will allow to go to the World Court. Beyond this lie problems which would seem to involve charter revision for a fairer system of representation of nations, the strengthening of power to arbitrate disputes, and the creation of a police force directly under its control.

There is also room for properly organized regional federations under the U. N., e.g., a United States of Europe and a developed Organization of American States, and for multinational agreements on trade, etc., but care should be taken that they do not conflict with a growth in the strength of the U. N. to deal with problems of universal importance. An interdependent world requires an inclusive world organization to supplant an anarchy of absolute nation-states or blocs formed by them. It is, to take an outstanding illustration, an idle dream to think that we can get properly controlled disarmament under a U. N. which does not include the effective government of China.

Disengagement

Since World War II the U. S. A. under a mixture of motives has assumed military obligations all over the world to contain communist expansion. Many of these commitments run beyond our wisdom or strength to maintain by military force at any price we can afford to pay. The President himself has wisely said that we were not omniscient or omnipotent, yet we tend to play that role around the world. Indeed, some of our programs, put forth in the name of fighting communism, actually help the Communists.

In Laos, the U. S. invested 300 million dollars in the support of an unpopular and corrupt regime. We purchased big cars for our friends, we supported a coup d'état, we drove Laotians who had been sympathetic to democracy toward the Pathet Lao. Likewise in South Vietnam we have backed the Diem regime which with its nepotism, its harassment of political opposition, and its forced removal of peasants from their villages, has been unable to carry on any kind of effective policy against the Viet Cong. In Laos the immediate situation requires the creation of an authentic neutralist regime whose integrity will be guaranteed by both power blocs. (*The peace arrangement between the Laotian factions was signed after this platform was adopted.*) In South Vietnam the U. S. must back democratic social reform and political freedom, not the Diem regime. We do not believe that America should "turn its back" on the people of Southeast Asia or of anywhere else. Rather we believe that a combined program of disarmament and social change, supported by the U. S., is the only meaningful alternative for the new states of the colonial revolution. We shall not serve democracy or peace by our engagement in protracted jungle war in Southeast Asia.

It is obvious on the one hand that many of these world crises would virtually disappear in a disarmed and federated world, and on the other that while they are acute they block emotionally and practically any substantial progress in disarmament negotiation. So closely tied are disarmament, disengagement and the strengthening of the U. N.

The question of Berlin is an example. It is right to defend the freedom of access to West Berlin. But war would mean almost certain destruction of the city. The one best chance of dealing with the problem of Berlin and Central Europe still lies in plans for demilitarizing Central Europe (like Austria) with phased withdrawals of troops on both sides. Both the Eisenhower and Kennedy administrations have summarily dismissed such plans and proceeded with the rearming of an originally reluctant West Germany whose Chancellor has become a serious threat to fruitful negotiation.

Our nation's most inexcusably dangerous commitment is to the absurdity that Chiang should still be recognized as president of China and entitled to represent her in the U. N. It is doubtful how justly he represents even Taiwan, where he has never risked a popular vote. He represents only the American Seventh Fleet.

In the light of such facts as these the Socialist Party demands of our government:

• The prompt beginning of negotiations looking to the seating on proper terms of the effective government of China in the U. N., and in the name of humanity an offer of food for the relief of famine. Proper terms would include some provision for Taiwan to determine its own status after peace prevails in the Far East. Meanwhile it could be represented in the U. N. as Taiwan.

• Guarantees against repetition of the Cuban debacle of military intervention in that country or in other Latin American nations.

• Re-examination of military commitments under all existing alliances or bilateral treaties, reports to the people on them and on the reasons for them, and plans for progressive disengagement from them.

• *Increased engagement in the holy war against unnecessary poverty, illiteracy, and illness in the world.* This is a matter of more money but not wholly of money. In terms of human service, the Socialist Party hails the work of the Peace Corps and of hundreds of Americans rendering similar services under nongovernmental agencies. We need men to use money well. Few responsible men in this field believe that more—if as much as —$10 billion of American money annually can now be wisely used under proper conditions.

Foreign Aid

In respect to financial aid, the Socialist Party urges that:

1. Aid should be strictly economic, not directed to military build-ups. It should be sufficient for its purposes. Too little aid may actually make conditions worse in a world where, despite considerable aid, the gap between the have and have-not nations has widened since World War II.

2. As far as possible the excellent mechanisms of the United Nations should be used.

3. Aid except in cases of relief or desperate hunger or disaster should be directed to specific economic developments to raise the standard of living of the masses.

4. All gifts and plans must be directed toward the upbuilding of the country and not to the strengthening of the governing elite of the military and landlords. Recipient nations should be required to set up special agencies capable of honest and efficient administration.

5. Where the economy of nations obviously suffers from terribly regressive taxation and a feudal land system effective reforms must be instituted as a condition of any worthwhile aid.

6. Where the problem of the population explosion in already overpopulated nations is serious, the recipient nations should be urged to make available proper means and facilities for birth control.

The 4th and 5th of these specifications on aid apply with special force to many of our Latin American neighbors. The President's Alliance for Progress is in general on sound ground, and properly carried out may yet atone for the American support so freely given in the past to dictators and corrupt governments in Latin America so long as they showed respect to capitalist interests of North American corporations. On its economic and political side we believe that the Alliance for Progress could be strengthened by the development of the Organization of American States. To its economic benefits should be added an arrangement to put some floor under prices of major Latin American agricultural and mineral exports. The prices of products such as coffee, sugar, tin and zinc have been subject to great fluctuation to the hurt of countries largely dependent upon those exports.

The economic problem in our world is not merely a problem of the two-thirds of humanity who live in bitter poverty. It is a problem of freer trade among all peoples. The Socialist Party supports President Kennedy's approach to this problem which has also, to its credit, been endorsed by the AFL-CIO. But we urge the importance of special consideration and assistance to workers displaced in some lines by the transition to freer trade.

To sum up this section on foreign policy: A distinction between foreign and domestic policy at this juncture in history is a matter of convenience of description rather than of essential differences in policy or principle. Politics—in the most inclusive sense of the word—does not and cannot stop at the waterfront. Not in a world which if it would live in peace and decency must give meaning to the truth that above all nations is humanity. Man by his own scientific skills has made it impossible to use great wars for other than the physical and spiritual destruction of humanity. This is the stark truth which now compels all men to work for a world with increasing cooperation and without war.

Socialism Re-examined

By

NORMAN THOMAS

From the perspective of the nuclear age, a great American re-examines the Socialist crusade which he has led for nearly forty years. Today socialism is caught between communism and modern democracy and finds itself loved by neither, yet socialist effort has been behind many of the great strides taken since the beginning of the century.

Although Mr. Thomas recalls socialism's failures and adjustments, he points to its many successes both hidden and proclaimed. He reviews the early days when its followers were fighting their way through a maze of revolutionary and reactionary ideologies in a time of social, economic and political ferment. He examines socialism as it has reacted to two world wars and now to the final, mandatory challenge of nuclear peace.

[Continued on back flap]

[Continued from front flap]

And he sees socialism against the inevitable moral decline of communism from idealism to pure power play.

In the end Mr. Thomas restates the socialist philosophy in terms of the changed world and finds it still the economic basis for the best solution to many of the world's greatest problems — the problems of an age sick with frustration, with little belief in progress, at war with itself on a dozen fronts, and with nationalism as its god.

"At this moment," he says, "if I looked from some distant planet on our struggles as one looks at a horse race, I should be inclined to bet on disaster, the triumph of ignorance, hate and greed. But I am not on a distant star. I have only my life to bet. Somehow through the ages we men have won for brotherhood victories which have kept our race alive and moving forward even when the odds against it were great. Our obliteration or our social damnation is not inexorably decreed by fate, not by our gods, not by our genes."